NO FEAR CODING

Computational Thinking
Across the K-5 Curriculum

HEIDI WILLIAMS

International Society for Technology in Education
PORTLAND, OREGON • ARLINGTON, VIRGINIA

No Fear Coding
Computational Thinking Across the K–5 Curriculum
Heidi Williams

Editor: *Emily Reed*
Copy Editor: *Kristin Landon*
Book Design and Production: *Jeff Puda*
Cover Design: *Edwin Ouellette*

Library of Congress Cataloging-in-Publication Data
Names: Williams, Heidi, author.
  Title: No fear coding : computational thinking across the K-5 curriculum /
    Heidi Williams.
  Description: Portland, Oregon : International Society for Technology in
    Education, [2017] | Includes bibliographical references.
  Identifiers: LCCN 2017015205 (print) | LCCN 2017024184 (ebook) | ISBN
    9781564846259 (mobi) | ISBN 9781564846266 (epub) | ISBN 9781564846273 (
    pdf) | ISBN 9781564843876 (pbk.)
  Subjects: LCSH: Computer science–Study and teaching (Elementary) | Computer
    programming–Study and teaching (Elementary)
  Classification: LCC QA76.27 (ebook) | LCC QA76.27 .W38 2017 (print) | DDC
    004.071–dc23
  LC record available at https://lccn.loc.gov/2017015205

First Edition
ISBN: 978-1-56484-387-6
Ebook version available.
Printed in the United States of America
ISTE® is a registered trademark of the International Society for Technology in Education.

About ISTE

The International Society for Technology in Education (ISTE) is the premier non-profit organization serving educators and education leaders committed to empowering connected learners in a connected world. ISTE serves more than 100,000 education stakeholders throughout the world.

ISTE's innovative offerings include the ISTE Conference & Expo, one of the biggest, most comprehensive edtech events in the world—as well as the widely adopted ISTE Standards for learning, teaching and leading in the digital age and a robust suite of professional learning resources, including webinars, online courses, consulting services for schools and districts, books, and peer-reviewed journals and publications. Visit iste.org to learn more.

Related ISTE Titles

Make, Learn, Succeed: Building a Culture of Creativity in Your School, by Mark Gura (2016)

To see all books available from ISTE, please visit iste.org/resources.

About the Author

 **Heidi Williams** is head of school for Jefferson Lighthouse, an IB (International Baccalaureate) Primary Years World School in Racine, Wisconsin. Williams is also known as the STRETCh (Striving to Reach Every Talented Child) Instructor **www.stretchinstructor.com** and has worked in the area of Gifted and Talented as a differentiation specialist and a K–12 GT Coordinator. She has a bachelor's degree in elementary education, a master's degree in curriculum and istruction, certificates in online teaching and coaching, and educational leadership licenses for principal and director of curriculum and instruction. She has presented at numerous local, state, and national conferences on the topics of differentiation and the use of technology to enhance learning. Her passions include the latest research in neuroscience and unlocking the doors of learning for students across the world. She lives in Wisconsin and has four beautiful daughters, as well as a devoted and loving husband.

Contributors

Catherine Castillo is a K–5 learning coach for Springfield Public Schools in Springfield, Missouri. She was a K–5 numeracy coach for six years and has served as a classroom teacher and a summer school administrator. Her passions are coding in the classroom, integration of STEM activities, and personalizing learning. Catherine holds master's degrees in curriculum and instruction and educational leadership. She regularly presents at local, state, and national conferences on a variety of math and STEM topics. Catherine lives in Springfield, Missouri with her two sons and their dog Isengard.

Vivian Chezvivian is Canadian-born, of Chinese descent, and currently living in Switzerland. She is an elementary school classroom generalist but has also taught as a music specialist, in ESL/EAL and also in Learning Support. She is a Coetail Post-Graduate Certificate grad and a former Coetail Coach. Her blog (**www.coetail. com/chezvivian**) curates her assignments for Coetail, her graduate studies in educational technology integration, and anything else education related that she feels inspired to write about.

Traci Kopeki is inspired to teach the whole student by using a variety of learning and technology platforms and incorporating students' differing learning styles. She would like to thank Heidi Williams for helping her open the doors to new ideas on learning. Not only has she been inspired to do this with her students, her three boys have kept her creatively thinking about how to learn in different ways. A fan of walking, biking, downhill skiing, and boating, Traci loves to get outside everyday. She lives in Wisconsin.

Karen North is a retired computer science, math, and career and technical education (CATE) teacher with 30 years' experience in public schools. She is a CS4TX.org leader, a Code.org affiliate, NCWIT Houston Aspirations coordinator, AAUW Expanding Your Horizons Conference coordinator, ISTE Computing Teachers Network officer, and a Code Buddy for Spring Branch ISD in Houston. Karen was honored as a White House Champion of Change for CS education in January 2016 for her advocacy work and online presence since 1985.

Acknowledgements

The author and editor would like to thank the contributors for their time and dedication and the many reviewers for their insightful comments. This book would not have been possible without the support and encouragement of Joseph Kmoch and the involvement of the ISTE Computing Teachers Network. This community actively works to encourage the teaching of computer science in PK–12 and to advance educators' skills and expertise in the area of computer science. To learn more about ISTE communities and membership visit **iste.org/join**.

Contents

Foreword

In his 2009 TED Talk, "How Great Leaders Inspire Action," Simon Sinek introduced a powerful model for inspirational leadership that begins with asking the "Why." He explains that most organizations and companies know what they do and how they do it, but less clear is why they do what they do. Simon discovered a pattern in how great leaders and organizations think, act, and communicate. He coined it the Golden Circle.

Using the Golden Circle, successful organizations begin by exploring the "Why"—the purpose, belief, or reason for doing something. The "Why" informs the processes we take to reach our desired result. Educators can employ this same thinking by asking themselves why they embarked on a career in education. Answers to this question will vary but might include things like, "to help students succeed in their lives and careers" or even, "to make the world a better place."

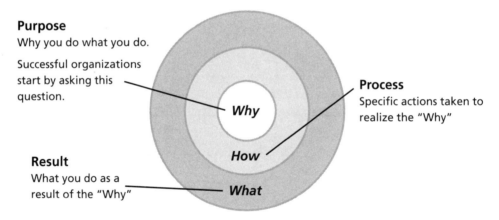

Figure F.1. Simon Sinek's Golden Circle.

Keeping the "Why" in mind, one can begin to explore from the inside out how to achieve teaching goals and what an effective instructional practice should look like.

No Fear Coding will start with why you should be teaching coding, how you can get it done without adding another thing to your day, and finally what you can do to bring coding and computational thinking skills into your existing curriculum and daily instruction.

Introduction

The Industrial Model of Education Must Change

Visualize a telephone from 100 years ago. Two months ago, I was in my father's basement with my daughter when she found an old rotary phone. She asked how it worked and began poking her finger into the round holes by each number. With her finger in one of the holes, I slowly rotated the dial around. She watched in awe as it returned to its original position. "Wow," she remarked. "You had to do that seven times before having it ring on the other end? Didn't that take, like, forever?"

Unlike the telephone, our educational system hasn't changed much from the classrooms of 100 years ago. This is expressed in "I Just Sued the School System," a YouTube video created by Prince EA in 2016 that has gone viral, receiving nearly six million views at the time of this printing (**youtu.be/dqTTojTija8**). The video contains a strong message for change, as the narrator calls "School" to the stand and accuses him of killing creativity and individuality. The "case" begins with images showing the changes in telephones and cars over the past century, and there is an audible gasp from the crowd when the image of a classroom from 100 years ago is compared one we see today. There is virtually no change.

For change in education to occur, we need to redefine what it means to be a teacher. The video challenges us to understand that the world has progressed and requires students who can think creatively, innovatively, critically, independently, and with the ability to connect. For their important role in shaping future leaders, the speaker argues that teachers should earn as much as doctors. Just as doctors treat each person as an individual and perform tests to determine what treatment will help improve their patient's health, teachers must help students improve their ability to process and use information. Learning to code and think computationally can help students master vital 21st century skills.

Education Is Moving from Teaching to Learning

Those who went into teaching twenty years ago studied subject matter and teaching methodologies and were often considered, and considered themselves, the holders of knowledge. With the availability of the internet, educators may no longer be the subject matter experts in the classroom. Students are constantly finding and engaging with—via Google searches, YouTube videos, and other methods—content they find interesting and have a passion for. In today's classroom, it is quite possible that a student knows more about a given topic than the teacher does.

Thanks to technology and the connectivity afforded by the internet and mobile devices, students no longer need to sit in a traditional classroom learn the same thing at the same time, all together. Students have access to tools such as Khan Academy, LearnZillion, Dreambox, IXL, and a variety of others to allow them to learn almost any subject they want to know more about. Gone are the days of having students leave school in June and return in September to "pick up right where they left off." Students now leave for the summer only to continue learning, exploring their passions, and gaining a whole new set of skills and background knowledge.

Changing our model of education involves shifting our focus from a teaching pedagogy to a learning pedagogy. In a teaching pedagogy, one asks oneself, "What should I teach?" compared to in a learning pedagogy where one asks, "What should my students be able to do with what they learn?" Both are important to the educational process and can be explained from the vantage point of the Golden Circle. Within this construct, teaching is the "How" (the process or delivery mechanism) and the "What" (the content delivered or knowledge imparted). Motivation becomes a key factor in learning, as this is the "Why" of the educational process.

Here is where coding becomes so important. Coding provides a vehicle for students to create content, rather than just consume it. For example, if a student has a passion for electricity and comes into your electricity unit with prior knowledge that is well beyond her peers, coding becomes a great avenue to allow the student to create with the content, rather than sit through lessons and consume content she already understands.

With the demand on teacher time to differentiate instruction for all learners, coding is a 21st century skill that naturally differentiates for its users. For example, there are at least five different ways to make a character move using coding. While none of these ways are wrong, students will naturally find ways that are more efficient the more they code.

Using This Book

This book will explore why you should be teaching coding and computational thinking, show how you can teach these skills using a variety of tools, and finally demonstrate what you can do now to add these skills into your existing curriculum and teaching.

The book is organized into sections featuring tools that can be used to integrate coding into the curriculum. Each section is laid out using three key concepts:

- The reason WHY using the resource within the curriculum will benefit students

- Description of HOW to get started with the resource

- Case studies and real world application of the resource showing WHAT you can do with it

What makes *No Fear Coding* different than other coding books or products is that it will not ask you to teach coding as a separate subject, but it will intentionally show teachers how to incorporate the skills of computer science within the instruction they already are responsible for covering. This book will challenge you to think computationally as you help students break down problems and create the thought processes needed to solve them.

No Fear!

The most important thing you can do is jump in and begin using the activities in this book. Activities and examples are paired with resources and Try It! challenges to deepen teacher understanding of the concepts explored in each section.

Teachers can use the information in this book to:

- Model risk taking.

- Use Bee-Bots to practice letters and numbers.

- Use Code.org to help young coders explore cardinal directions (up, down, right, left).

- Use Scratch to create a video game demonstrating knowledge on electricity.

- Use Scratch to "play" with the concept of estimation.

- Use ARIS to create a walking tour of your community.

- Incorporate coding activities into teaching the Standards for Mathematical Practice.

Table 0.1 outlines four tools featured in this book that you can use to begin your journey into coding.

The website for this book (**Nofearcoding.org**) contains worksheets and rubrics for lesson within the book, as well as links to resources and projects.

TABLE 0.1. Coding Resources and Where to Find Them

RESOURCE	WHAT IS IT?	WHAT DOES IT LOOK LIKE?	WHERE DO I FIND IT?
Bee-Bots	A Bee-Bot is a programmable floor robot intended for use by young children. Its design and interface appeals to young students and offers a perfect starting point for teaching control, directional language, and programming.		**bee-bot.us**
Code.org	Code.org is a non-profit dedicated to expanding access to computer science and increasing participation by women and underrepresented minorities. Code.org makes learning how to code accessible through lessons, videos, and other resources on its website.		**code.org**
Scratch	Scratch is a visual programming language learners of all ages can use to create interactive stories, games, and animations. Scratch helps young people learn to think creatively, reason systematically, and work collaboratively — essential skills for life in the digital age.		**scratch.mit.edu**
ARIS	ARIS is a user-friendly, open-source platform for creating and engaging with mobile games, tours, and interactive stories. Using GPS and QR codes, ARIS players experience a hybrid world of virtual interactive characters, items, and media placed in physical space.		**arisgames.org**

Coding and Computational Thinking

Technology has changed how we do things, from reading a book to talking to others, and our ability to use data and computing technology can greatly improve lives when people use them to find innovative solutions to everyday problems. This section explores the "Why" for teaching coding—and the underlying skill of computational thinking—and shows how it can be integrated into existing curriculum. You will learn:

- The five reasons why coding is critical for K–5 students
- What computational thinking means
- How to teach coding and computational thinking across the curriculum

Why Should K–5 Educators Teach Coding?

It's time we realize and put to action Steve Job's words: "Everyone in this country should learn how to program a computer...because it teaches you how to think." This quote appears at the beginning of a video entitled "What Most School Don't Teach" (**youtu.be/nKIu9yen5nc**) that was published in 2013 by Code.org. Starring many famous people, including Bill Gates of Microsoft, Mark Zuckerberg of Facebook, and will.i.am of the Black-Eyed Peas, the video's message is a simple one: anyone and everyone should learn to code.

Within our schools, we must build upon the belief that coding is for everyone. There are many reasons for teaching coding, among them:

• It's about teaching perseverance.

• It's about teaching students how to think and reason (computational thinking).

• It's about creativity and expression.

• It's another way to demonstrate content knowledge (just like creating a Power-Point or display board).

• It's a way to see math in action.

Coding Is for Everyone, and Parents Agree!

Code.org is a non-profit organization dedicated to giving every student in every school the opportunity to learn computer programming. An article published on the Code.org blog *Anybody Can Learn* reports that of all the new wages within the U.S., only 16% are in computer science (Code.org, 2016).

The Bureau of Labor Statistics data on mean salaries showed the average salary across all occupations is $48,320, while the average salary across computing jobs is $86,170. They also acknowledge that the computer science field is growing faster than other fields, and so they expect the number to grow. The average "demand rate" (online ads divided by current employment) is 14.8% for computing categories, and 3.8% on average across all other jobs (Code.org, 2016).

The article also shared the scary statistic that in 2014, only 42,969, or two and a half percent of all bachelor's degrees were earned in computer science. Why aren't more university students studying computer science? One reason is because students don't learn about this field in grades K–12, despite evidence that early exposure is highly correlated to majoring in computer science.

The solution proposed in the article is for schools to teach computer science in grades K–12 and, according to a survey Code.org conducted, 90% of parents agree.

Five Reasons Why Coding Is Critical for K–5 Students

1. Making Their Thinking Visible

We know that young students are concrete thinkers and are beginning to follow step-by-step directions. These beginning stages of following first one step, then two steps, then multiple steps, are the start of algorithmic thinking in action. While the youngest learners may not understand this abstract concept, we can use computer science to make their thinking visible.

One of the behaviors of good readers is to visualize the story in their mind as they are reading. Students often struggle to work in reverse and put their thoughts into writing, as they cannot see them. By learning how to code, students have an opportunity to give shapes, thoughts, and actions to their thinking.

2. Sustaining Creativity

In Sir Ken Robinson's TED Talk, "Do Schools Kill Creativity?" the renowned educator and speaker tells the audience that creativity is as important in education as literacy. He points out that young learners will take a chance and are not afraid to be wrong. As we get older, he says, adults lose their capacity for creativity because they are afraid of being wrong (Robinson, 2006).

Coding allows students to be creative without being wrong. If something doesn't work, the student must analyze what isn't working, ask why it isn't working, and determine how to correct it so that it works. In essence, coding is the process of continually making mistakes, learning from them, and correcting them.

3. Encouraging Computational Thinking

As a teacher, how many times have you heard the following feedback? *"Johnny is great at solving computational math problems, but he continues to struggle with word problems."*

Teaching how to read and write code supports a student's ability to think computationally. To make breakthroughs in teaching students how to solve word problems, we must help them understand how their brains work—like a highly complex computer. This process involves breaking apart a problem (Decomposition), identifying and creating the steps needed to solve the problem (Algorithms & Procedures), running the procedures (Data Collection), analyzing the results (Data Analysis) and determining if the results yielded an acceptable answer (Data Representation & Abstraction).

Our world continually presents us with roadblocks that, given the correct framework of thinking, have solutions that can harness the power of technology to make a difference in the world. Jeanette Wing defines computational thinking as "the thought processes involved in formulating problems and their solutions so that the solutions are represented in a form that can be efficiently carried out by an information-processing agent" (Wing, 2006). For the classroom teacher, this means they must look at the students' brain as the information-processing agent.

4. Fostering Future-Ready Skills

The Partnership for 21st Century Learning (P21) developed a framework describing the "skills, knowledge and expertise students should master to succeed in work and life in the 21st century (Partnerhip for 21st Century Learning, 2007)." The framework identified three learning and innovation skills essential in preparing our children for increasingly complex life and work environments that don't yet exist. These skills, often referred to as the 4 C's, are critical thinking, communication, collaboration, and creativity.

Collaboration and communication are rapidly changing with the use of technology. We can now collaborate by communicating across the state, country, and world in real time. Working on a project and receiving instant feedback, due to advances in computer programming, has pushed us into needing a workforce that can think computationally.

Creativity and critical thinking can be used with coders of all ages. Coding allows the user to become the creator of content, rather than just the consumer of content. When we consume content we are learning about the "What" and the "How," but when we create content we have engaged the "Why" of learning.

5. Empowering Students to Take Action

Coding is about applying skills and creativity to solve problems. For example, in the winter of 2011, a group of young coders were stuck in Boston during a snow storm. Their task was to create a new website for Boston's Public Schools; however, within days of their arrival the city had shut down. What resulted was the coders creating a website called Adopt a Hydrant (adoptahydrant.org) that allowed area residents to adopt a fire hydrant and keep it clear of snow for emergency personnel during the winter months.

Coding can be used to create real-world contexts for students. When we blur the lines between school and the real world, we allow children to examine problems, engage them in exploring the problems, and empower them to take action in finding a solution.

Many people think action is something you do and is therefore easy to define; however, if we go back to the Golden Circle, we recognize that action stems from the reason why we do something. If we want children to make a difference in the world, we need to help them understand that action is not a mandate from parents or teachers, but a lifelong mindset that teachers and parents can help develop. It must be developed with scaffolded lessons that include explicitly taught skills, modeled behaviors, and a gradual release of responsibility.

The following teacher reflection questions can help you begin to think about the process:

- What is inquiry's relationship to action?

- How does computational thinking support the skills needed to take action?

- How can technology be used to record, assess, and report on action?

• How do coding skills fit into one's ability to take action?

Why *Not* Teach Coding?

While there are many reasons for adding coding, there are an equal or greater number of arguments against. The first step to incorporating coding into existing curriculum is to identify the roadblocks.

Roadblock 1: *Getting Comfortable with Living in Beta*

In many schools across the country there are after school clubs dedicated to computer science and coding. While this is a great start for exposure, it does not allow all students to access the computational thinking skills that are developed by coding. Teachers who have a passion for computer science are usually the ones running these clubs, but how do we get *all* K-5 teachers comfortable with coding?

This brings us to the ability to live in beta. This concept is explored by Molly Schroeder in her 2013 TED talk "Living in Beta" (youtube.com/watch?v=0nnYI3ePrY8). Schroder defines beta as "the space between A and B" and adds that this is where the learning happens. She points out that with the ever-changing nature of technology, we would best serve our students by jumping in with them as they approach solving a problem. New discoveries in neuro-science and revelations on how the brain works are changing the way teachers interact with student learning opportunities. Coding is a new literacy that is upon us and, as she states in her TED Talk, "if we sit around waiting until it all shakes out, we're going to miss the boat. Not only will we be too late and learn nothing along the way, but we'll also lose out on the opportunity to help influence how things evolve and take shape (Schroeder, 2013)."

Roadblock 2: *Fear of Failure*

Often I have heard K-5 teachers say, "but I can't do that without a lot of professional development." Teachers may fear the unknown and feel they don't understand, or have time to learn, how to code. More importantly, the field of education has an overall fear of failing, spreading to the paralyzing fear of risk-taking. This is our biggest hurdle! Allowing teachers to take risks, fail, and learn to improve the process from their failure is what coding is all about.

The essential question becomes, how do we get off this escalator we are stuck on? Take a moment to watch the YouTube video "Stuck on An Escalator-Take Action" (**youtu.be/VrSUe_m19FY**). It shows two people who are literally stuck on an escalator when it stops moving. When I showed this to a group of teachers, they all laughed as the lady asks the gentleman stuck on the escalator with her for a cell phone. The gentleman then proceeds to shout, "Hello...there are two people stuck on an escalator and we need help...now! Would somebody please do something?" The two proceed to sit down on their respective steps until a repair technician comes to fix the escalator, only to get stuck about half way up the escalator. The video concludes by stating that most problems are easy to solve, you just need to get off the escalator. In order to get off our escalator and face our fear of coding, we need to understand the Law of Diffusion of Innovation and how it relates to coding in K-5.

Everett Rogers, a professor of communication studies, popularized this theory in his book *Diffusion of Innovations* in 1962. The book has since been revised and the fifth edition was published in 2003. The basis of the theory is that diffusion is the process by which an innovation is communicated over time among an organization. According to Rogers' theory, there are five categories of those who adopt an innovation.

> **Innovators.** Individuals who are willing to take risks, have financial backing, and have scientific resources and interaction with other innovators, all of which allows them to adopt innovations that may ultimately fail.

> **Early Adopters.** Those who have the highest degree of opinion leadership and advanced education. They are more cautious in adoption choices than the innovators.

> **Early Majority.** Those who will adopt an innovation after a degree of time in which they have seen its successful use. This group usually has above average social status, but this group is not seen as having opinion leadership.

> **Late Majority.** Those who approach an innovation with skepticism.

> **Laggards.** The last group to adopt the innovation. This group of individuals typically has an aversion to change.

The innovators of the K-5 Coding include Seymore Papert, Michel Resnick, Fred Martin, and others who developed and adopted early programming languages; beginning in the 1970s with Logo, which was used to draw shapes, designs, and patterns by typing in simple commands on the screen; and leading to the development of Scratch, a visual block programming language made specifically for young coders, in 2004.

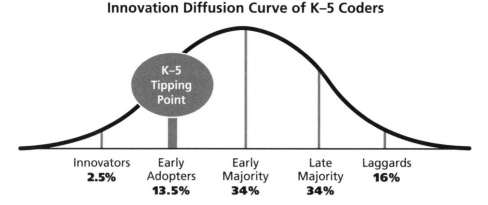

Figure 1.1. Innovation diffusion curve showing rate
of adoption of coding by K-5 students.

The early adopters began catching on to these coding platforms and coding grew in popularity throughout the first decade of the 21st Century. In 2004, the Computer Science Teachers Association (CSTA) was founded and it created recommended computer science standards. Coding gained more popularity though collaborative social platforms like the one created for Scratch (**scratch.mit.edu**) in 2012. Hadi Partovi followed suit and launched Code.org in 2013. Each year, Code.org organizes the Hour of Code, which, according to their 2016 Annual Report, has engaged more than 350 million students, reaching one out of every ten children on the planet (Code.org, 2017).

Figure 1.1 shows the tipping point that Code.org hopes to achieve through the coding resources they provide for students and educators.

By picking up this book, and trying out at least one activity, you will be an early adopter by bringing coding into the curriculum and fostering development of this important 21st century literacy in your school!

Roadblock 3: *Time*

For K-5 teachers to incorporate coding and computational thinking, we simply cannot add another subject to their already full schedules. Teachers are already tasked with creating learning experiences in reading, writing, science, social studies, health, and habits of mind. How can they be expected to add learning and teaching coding to their schedules?

What teachers may not realize is that they are already teaching many of the foundational components of computational thinking. When we ask students to read a story and then sequence the events into the correct order, they are using the same process a computer programmer uses in decomposition, data analysis, and data representation. For example, when computer programmers are presented with a complex problem to solve, they first need to break the problem down into simple parts. Then the programmer will analyze the parts and put them in the correct order. Finally, the computer will represent the data in a simple way that the user can understand. Our youngest readers use this same process when the teacher reads them a story and they must take the picture representation of the story and put it into the correct sequence of events to make meaning. It is not more time we need, but the ability to help our students make the connections.

The required skills within the Common Core State Standards and particularly the Standards for Mathematical Practice can be taught using coding as a tool. I often hear of teachers struggling to find concrete ways to teach and observe these eight mathematics standards. Appendix B shares connections between computational thinking and the Standards for Mathematical Practice, and strategies for implementing coding within the math classroom. Again, it is not a matter of adding more time to another subject, but using a 21st century tool in a way that will help the concrete understanding of often time abstract mathematical concepts.

Coding = Computational Thinking

How does coding = computational thinking? Since computational thinking is all about the thought processes needed to think like a computer, the use of coding allows students to think computationally and receive immediate feedback on their thinking. Thus, coding can be seen as computational thinking without human error.

For example, if a student is thinking computationally about the steps needed to draw a square, she could write them down on a piece of paper and have a partner try to follow her directions. This process however is open to error. The person interpreting the directions might do so incorrectly. However, if the student put her computational thinking into a coding language (such as Scratch), she could run the program and check to see if her thinking was correct. If the program runs correctly, her thinking is validated. If the program does not run correctly, she knows there was an error in her thinking.

Since our understanding is built upon our prior knowledge, exposure to new learning experiences (input), is followed by modifying and clarifying new thinking to create meaning (process), then followed by the new learning we have constructed (output), to finally receive information on the expected results (feedback).

Computational Thinking Defined

The International Society for Technology in Education (ISTE), in collaboration with the Computer Science Teachers Association (CSTA), developed an operational definition of computational thinking for K–12 Education. The purpose behind this work was to provide a framework and vocabulary that would resonate with educators. ISTE and CSTA gathered feedback from nearly 700 computer science teachers, researchers, and practitioners who showed overwhelming support of the definition.

Computational thinking is a problem-solving process that includes (but is not limited to) the following characteristics:

- Formulating problems in a way that enables us to use a computer and other tools to help solve them

- Logically organizing and analyzing data

- Representing data through abstractions such as models and simulations

- Automating solutions through algorithmic thinking (a series of ordered steps)

- Identifying, analyzing, and implementing possible solutions with the goal of achieving the most efficient and effective combination of steps and resources

- Generalizing and transferring this problem solving process to a wide variety of problems (ISTE & CSTA, 2011)

More importantly, these skills lead to the following dispositions or attitudes:

- Confidence in dealing with complexity

- Persistence in working with difficult problems

- Tolerance for ambiguity

- The ability to deal with open-ended problems

- The ability to communicate and work with others to achieve a common goal or solution (ISTE & CSTA, 2011)

Components of Computational Thinking

While there are many websites and resources that contain a breakdown of computational thinking concepts, Table 2.1 shares the computational thinking concepts and definitions created by ISTE and CSTA in their computational thinking vocabulary and progression chart.

TABLE 1.1. Computational Thinking (CT) Vocabulary Chart

COMPUTATIONAL THINKING CONCEPTS	DEFINITION
Data Collection	The process of gathering appropriate information.
Data Analysis	Making sense of data, finding patterns, and drawing conclusion.
Data Representation	Depicting and organizing data in appropriate graphs, charts, words or images
Problem Decomposition	Breaking down tasks into smaller, manageable parts.
Abstraction	Reducing complexity to define main idea.
Algorithms & Procedures	Series of ordered steps taken to solve a problem or achieve some end.
Automation	Having computers or machines do repetitive or tedious tasks.
Simulation	Representation or model of a process. Simulation also involves running experiments using models.
Parallelization	Organize resources to simultaneously carry out tasks reach a common goal.

Computational Thinking, Project Based Learning, and Inquiry Based Learning

Rather than looking at each item as a separate entity, looking through the lens of project based and inquiry based learning will help us better understand how to put these skills in context for our students. With the popularity of project based learning (or PBL), many schools are beginning to use this learning model. Figure 2.4 looks at the crossover between PBL, computational thinking, and inquiry based learning. This graphic was created from the most common concepts and vocabulary across a study of five of the most commonly used project based and inquiry based learning models.

What can be learned by this comparison is that the process of inquiry, investigation, and research can be complex. Many K-5 teachers struggle with how to explicitly teach these skills to students. This is where computational thinking can come in handy! Reducing the complexity of a problem by breaking the steps of inquiry into a smaller series of ordered steps, to gather the information and make sense of it, to draw conclusions, and to represent the data using graphs, charts, words, and images is computational thinking in action.

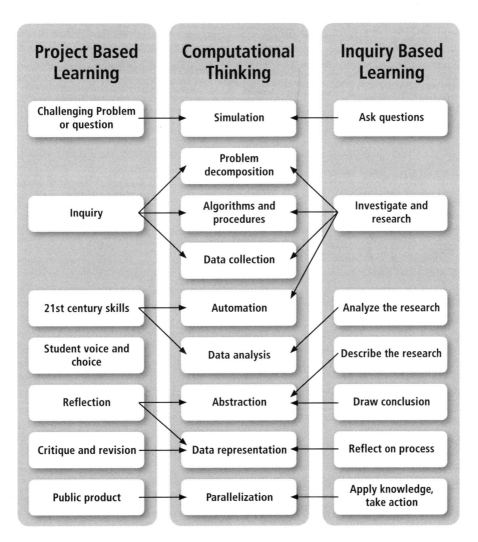

Figure 2.1. This graphic shows how project based learning and inquiry based learning both feed into computational thinking.

Imagine a K–5 classroom where steps are intentionally taught to decompose complex problems into simple tasks that can be completed by a group of students collaborating with each other. Now those would be employable students who have the 21st century skill set to be college and career ready for jobs that do not yet exist!

Special note should be given to how inquiry, investigation, and research can be broken down into distinct computational thinking concepts that can intentionally be taught in the classroom.

This understanding of computational thinking will help educators better understand how to break apart the Common Core State Standards involving research. For example, Common Core State Standard CCSS.ELA-Literacy in the area of "Research to Build and Present Knowledge," is broken down by grade level as follows:

ELA-Literacy.W.K.7: Participate in shared research and writing projects (e.g., explore a number of books by a favorite author and express opinions about them).

ELA-Literacy.W.1.7: Participate in shared research and writing projects (e.g., explore a number of "how-to" books on a given topic and use them to write a sequence of instructions).

ELA-Literacy.W.2.7: Participate in shared research and writing projects (e.g., read a number of books on a single topic and produce a report; record science observations).

ELA-Literacy.W.3.7: Conduct short research projects that build knowledge about a topic.

ELA-Literacy.W.4.7: Conduct short research projects that build knowledge through investigation of different aspects of a topic.

ELA-Literacy.W.5.7: Conduct short research projects that use several sources to build knowledge through investigation of different aspects of a topic.

Resources for Learning More about Computational Thinking

Google offers a free course for educators called "Computational Thinking for Educators." The course breaks down and provides content examples in application. The goal of the course is to expose educators to computational thinking and help them understand the differences between computational thinking and computer science. Often, K–5 teachers think that Computational Thinking and Computer Science are one in the same. The reality is that they are extremely different.

The course is user friendly and introduces the "Exploring Algorithms" unit be making an analogy with the popular game Twenty Questions. Elementary students love to play this game, and teachers have integrated many different renditions of the game with their content areas. This helps K–5 educators build from the known in the understanding of computational thinking.

The course is divided into five units:

Introducing Computational Thinking: What is computational thinking, where does it occur, why should you care, and how is it being applied?

Exploring Algorithms: Walk through examples of algorithms used in your subject area. Recognize why algorithms are powerful tools to increase what you can do and that technology can be useful for implementing and automating algorithms.

Finding Patterns: Explore examples of patterns in various patterns in various subjects and develop your own processes for approaching a problem through pattern recognition.

Developing Algorithms: Increase your confidence in applying the computational process to a given problem and recognize how algorithms can articulate a process or rule.

Final Project: Applying Computational Thinking: Create a statement of how computational thinking applies to your subject area and plan to integrate it into your work and classroom.

 Try it! Complete the Google Computational Thinking course and share your final project at **Nofearcoding.org**.

CHAPTER

3

How Does Coding Fit into Curriculum?

I n 2013, the Computer Science Teachers Association (CSTA) published a report titled "Bugs in the System," outlining steps that could be taken to help school districts integrate coding into the curriculum. The report noted that the U.S. educational system is highly decentralized when it comes to decision making, as standards can be set at the state, district, or even school level. Countries such as England and Finland, where educational policies are set and enforced at the national level, made addressing computer science skills more succinct. While national-level efforts are being made to formalize standards in some "core" subjects as math and literacy, this is not the case for Computer Science (CSTA & ACM, 2013).

Integrating Coding into the Curriculum

One way to help address computer science is to view it not as a technical subject that needs to be taught, but rather a language that continues to evolve over time. For our youngest learners, coding will be viewed as just another language. According to Mitchel Resnick, professor at the MIT Media Lab, "Coding is the new literacy. To thrive in tomorrow's society, young people must learn to design, create and express themselves with digital technologies (Berkman Klein Center, 2014)." In

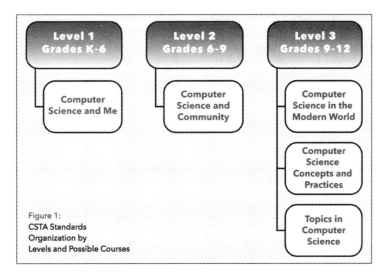

Figure 3.1. Organizing structure for the Computer Science Standards. Graphic reprinted with permission from CSTA's document "Bugs in the System: Computer Science Teacher Certification in the U.S.

an article posted on the Connections Academy blog titled "Why Learning to Code Benefits Kids, Regardless of Future Career Choice," Linda Liukas, the founder of an all-girls coding organization called Rails Girls is quoted as saying, "I don't think everyone will be a coder, but the ability to speak and structure your thinking in a way a computer understands it will be one of the core future skills[,] whatever your field (Werrell, 2014)."

CSTA Standards

To address this need, the CSTA worked to create and is constantly updating a set of standards that cover all grade levels. The CSTA K–12 Computer Science Standards (CSTA, 2011) clearly defined, for use by any state or school district, the framework for grade-appropriate standards underpinning K–12 Computer Science education. This framework focused on fundamental concepts and had the following general goals:

1. The curriculum should prepare students to understand the nature of computer science and its place in the modern world.

2. Students should understand that computer science includes principles, skills, insights, and perspectives.

3. Students should be able to use computer science concepts (especially algorithmic/computational thinking) in their problem-solving activities in other subjects (for example, the use of logic for understanding the semantics of English in a language arts class).

4. The Computer Science curriculum should complement information technology and AP computer science curricula in schools where they are currently offered.

The basis of this book is Level 1: Computer Science and Me (recommended for grades K–6). At this level, elementary school students are introduced to foundational concepts in computer science by integrating basic skills in technology with simple ideas about computational thinking. The learning experiences created from these standards should be inspiring and engaging, helping students see computing as an important part of their world. They should be designed with a focus on active learning, creativity, and exploration and will often be embedded within other curricular areas such as social science, language arts, mathematics, and science.

When developing the new standards, the CSTA looked to the components of the K–12 Computer Science Framework. This framework was built upon the knowledge that standards are built from what students know and can do. These two components of knowing and doing are what make up a standard.

This is an essential component for educators to understand, as our industrialized model of education focused on the *knowing* rather than the *doing*. By focusing on having students demonstrate the knowing *and* doing, we are creating performance expectations that our students must demonstrate. This type of assessment is not something that is multiple choice or even short essay. Performance assessments provide us with evidence that document student understanding and thinking through their ability to perform a task.

ISTE Standards for Students

The ISTE standards have been evolving since 1998. In 1998, the journey began by understanding and learning how to use technology. Almost ten years later, the 2007 standards shifted to using technology to learn. The latest edition of the 2016 ISTE Standards for Students pushes educators to transform learning with the use of technology.

Standard 5, Computational Thinker, states: "Students develop and employ strategies for understanding and solving problems in ways that leverage the power of technological methods to develop and test solutions (ISTE, 2016)."

Standard 5 is broken down into the following five indicators:

5a. Students formulate problem definitions suited for technology-assisted methods such as data analysis, abstract models and algorithmic thinking in exploring andfinding solutions.

5b. Students collect data or identify relevant data sets, use digital tools to analyze them, and represent data in various ways to facilitate problem-solving and decision-making.

5c. Students break problems into component parts, extract key information and develop descriptive models to understand complex systems or facilitate problem-solving.

5d. Students understand how automation works and use algorithmic thinking to develop a sequence of steps to create and test automated solutions. (ISTE, 2016)

K–5 students need to learn how computing tools can be used to help solve problems, communicate with others, and access and organize information by themselves or in collaboration with others. They must also learn to be responsible citizens in the ever-changing digital world. It is important to recognize the significant impact that an early exposure to the ISTE Standards for Students can have in truly redefining the way in which we deliver instruction.

Correlation to Standards

Table 3.1 contains PK through second grade examples from the computational thinking vocabulary chart in Chapter 2. The alignment to Common Core State Standards (CCSS), 2016 ISTE Standards for Students, and Next Generation Science Standards (NexGen) has been included to help educators see how they can implement into the curriculum they are already teaching.

TABLE 3.1. Computational Thinking (CT) Progression Chart for PK – 2

ISTE / CSTA COMPUTATIONAL THINKING CONCEPTS	GRADES PK–2	STANDARDS CORRELATION
Data Collection	Conduct an experiment to find the fastest toy car down an incline and record the order of cars across the finish line.	**NGSS.K–2-ETS1, ETS2, ETS3**
Data Analysis	Make generalizations about the order of finishing a toy car race based on the characteristics of the car with a focus on weight. Test conclusions by adding weight to cars to change results.	**CCSS.ELA-Literacy.W.2.6, W.2.8**
Data Representation	Create a chart of line drawing that shows how the speed of a toy car changes when its weight is changed.	**CCSS.Math. Content.2. MD.D.10**
Problem Decomposition	Create directions to a location in the school by breaking the directions into smaller geographical zones. Join the sections of directions together into a whole.	**CCSS.Math. Content.2. MD.D.10**
Abstraction	With many sizes and colors of three-sided shapes, the abstract is a triangle.	**CCSS.Math. Content.1. G.A.1**
Algorithms & Procedures	Create a set of directions from the school to the major landmarks in the neighborhood.	**CCSS.ELA-Literacy.W.1.2, W.2.2**
Automation	Converse with a classroom in another state or country to learn about their culture using Internet-based tools to replace writing letters.	**ISTE Student Standards 6, 7**
Simulation	After a set of directions has been created, act out the steps to be sure they are correct.	**CCSS.ELA-Literacy.SL.2.4**
Parallelization	Based on a set of criteria, break the class into two groups. Have one group read aloud while the other group provides humming background music. The goal is reached, but the whole is better than the individual parts.	**CCSS.ELA-Literacy.SL.2.1**

Table 3.2 contains third through fifth grade examples from the original chart in Appendix C. The alignment to Common Core State Standards (CCSS), 2016 ISTE Standards for Students, and Next Generation Science Standards (NexGen) has been included to help educators see how they can implement into the curriculum they are already teaching.

TABLE 3.2. Computational Thinking (CT) Progression Chart for 3-5

ISTE / CSTA COMPUTATIONAL THINKING CONCEPTS	GRADES 3–5	STANDARDS CORRELATION
Data Collection	Review examples of writing to identify strategies for writing an essay.	**Writing Standards 1,2, and 3**
Data Analysis	Categorize strong and weak examples of writing samples to develop a rubric.	**ELA Writing and Language Standards**
Data Representation	Match each writing sample to the rubric and create a chart showing which example best fits each category of the rubric.	**CCSS.ELA-Literacy.W.3.4, W.4.4, W.5.4**
Problem Decomposition	Develop a plan to make the school "green." Separate strategies such as recycling paper and cans, reducing use of electricity, and composting food waste.	**NGSS.4-ESS3-1**
Abstraction	Hear a story, reflect on main items, and determine an appropriate title.	**CCSS.ELA-Literacy.RL.5.2**
Algorithms & Procedures	Design a board game and write instruction to play. Test instructions on peers trying to play the game. Refine instructions with feedback from peers who played the game.	**CCSS.ELA-Literacy.W.3.2, W.3.5, W.4.2, W.4.5, W.5.2, W.5.5**
Automation	Investigate what automation is through real-world examples like barcodes, teller machines, and library bar codes.	**ISTE Student Standard 5d**

Table continues on following page.

27

ISTE / CSTA COMPUTATIONAL THINKING CONCEPTS	GRADES 3–5	SRANDARDS CORRELATION
Simulation	Create an animation to demonstrate understanding of the process.	**NGSS- Engineering Design**
Parallelization	Teachers facilitate in planning team project timelines, roles and assignments and working together to complete components (how do we break up the tasks, what tasks have to be done sequentially and others simultaneously, check ins, meeting deadlines?).	**P21 21st Century Skills: Collaboration & Cooperation**

Computational Thinking Across the Curriculum

In 2009, ISTE and CSTA created a document titled "Computational Thinking Across the Curriculum" to identify core computational thinking concepts and capabilities. The matrix they created provides examples of activities that span a variety of content areas, showing how computational thinking can be incorporated into any subject you are teaching. Table 3.3 includes activities mapped to computational thinking concepts that can be done as stand-alone projects.

TABLE 3.3. Computational thinking concepts and capabilities across content areas.

CT CONCEPT	COMPUTER SCIENCE	MATH	SCIENCE	LANGUAGE	SOCIAL STUDIES
Data Collection	Find a data source for a problem area.	Find a data source for a problem area (flipping coins, throwing dice).	Collect data from an experiment.	Study battle statistics or population data.	Do linguistic analysis of sentences.

CT CONCEPT	COMPUTER SCIENCE	MATH	SCIENCE	LANGUAGE	SOCIAL STUDIES
Data Analysis	Write a program to do basic statistical calculations on a set of data.	Count occurrences of coin flips or dice throws and analyze results.	Analyze data from an experiment.	Identify trends in data from statistics.	Identify patterns for different sentence types.
Data Representation	Use data structures such as array, linked list, stack, etc…	Use histogram, pie chart, bar chart to represent data; use sets, lists, graphs, to contain data	Summarize data from an experiment.	Summarize and represent trends.	Represent patterns of different sentence types.
Problem Decomposition	Define objects and methods; define main and functions.	Apply order of operations in an expression.	Do a species classification.		Write an outline.
Abstraction	Use procedures to complete a set of often repeated commands that perform a function.	Use variables in Algebra; identify essential facts in a word problem; …use iteration to solve word problems.	Build a model of a physical entity.	Summarize facts; deduce conclusions from facts.	Use of simile and metaphor; write a story with branches.

Table continues on following page.

CT CONCEPT	COMPUTER SCIENCE	MATH	SCIENCE	LANGUAGE	SOCIAL STUDIES
Algorithms and Procedures	Study or implement an algorithm for a problem area.	Do long division, factoring; do carries in addition or subtraction.	Do an experimental procedure.		Write instructions.
Automation		Use tools such as Geometer, Sketch Pad.	Use Probeware.	Use Excel.	Use a spell checker.
Parallelization	Divide up data or task in such a way to be processed in parallel.	Solve linear systems; do matrix multiplication.	Run experiments with different parameters at the same time.		
Simulation	Use an algorithm or animation,	Graph a function and modify values of variables.	Simulate movement of the solar system.	Play Oregon Trail.	Do a re-enactment from a story.

The language in the original document was slightly modified to better apply to K–5 teachers. Some of the technical vocabulary and concepts meant for higher levels have been eliminated. The original document can be found at **goo.gl/wcLNks**.

Other resources share ideas on how to teach computational thinking skills, but *No Fear Coding* takes a different look at computational thinking. Helping K–5 teachers understand they are already using many of these skills and concepts within their curriculum requires a holistic view of computational thinking.

What Teaching Coding Looks Like

Many of the available coding and computational thinking resources can seem overwhelming to the K–5 classroom teacher. For those schools who are lucky enough to have a K–5 computer science teacher, these resources might seem exciting to integrate into their class. However, the vast majority of K–5 schools do not have such positions and so the task of integrating coding falls to the classroom teacher who may or may not have computer science experience.

For the average K–5 teacher, one look at the code written in the Google lesson plan on the present participle in Figure 4.1 and the teacher quickly closes the website. The use of actual code and programming languages such as Python can be intimidating for someone new to coding. The concept that Google applies for computational thinking is instructionally sound, it just needs to be simplified if we hope to get our K–5 classroom teachers "off the escalator."

Once completed, the program should be able to: Check to see if the last letter is 'e'. If it is, Python will take all the letters except the last letter ('e') and add 'ing' to the end. Otherwise, Python will just add 'ing' to the end without dropping any letters.

```
my_verb = raw_input('Please enter a verb: ')
def drop_e(verb):
 if verb[-1] == 'e':
   pres_part = _____ + 'ing'
   print 'The last letter is "e".'
   print 'Drop the ending "e" before adding "ing".'
   print 'present participle:', pres_part
 else:
   pres_part = _____ + 'ing'
   print 'The last letter is not "e".'
   print 'Add "ing".'
   print 'present participle:', pres_part
drop_e(my verb)
```

Figure 4.1. Google lesson plan on present participle.

How do we take the fear out of coding for K–5 teachers who must spend the majority of their time on reading, writing, and math skills? This is where *No Fear Coding* simplifies the process and makes it K–5 teacher friendly. Compare the Google lesson in Figure 4.1 to the *No Fear Coding* lesson that displays the same content in a more K–5 teacher- and student-friendly format (Figure 4.2).

When you look at Figure 4.2, the visual block programming makes the program steps easier to "read" and to understand without needing to know Python or other coding languages.

Starting at the top of the coding blocks, the program reads:

1. When the green flag is clicked, the program will run.

2. The program will ask "Does your verb end with an 'e'?" and will wait for your answer.

3. If the answer is "yes" then the computer will think, "then I will need to take the 'e' off the end of the verb."

4. The program will ask "What is the verb without the 'e' on the end?" and wait.

5. The program will take the answer and join "ing" to it. So if you entered "mak" for "make," the Scratch cat would say "making."

6. If the answer to the first question "Does your verb end with an 'e'?" was no, the program will skip down to the "else" statement, ask, "What is the verb?" and then join "ing" to the answer. So if you answered "sing," the Scratch cat would say "singing."

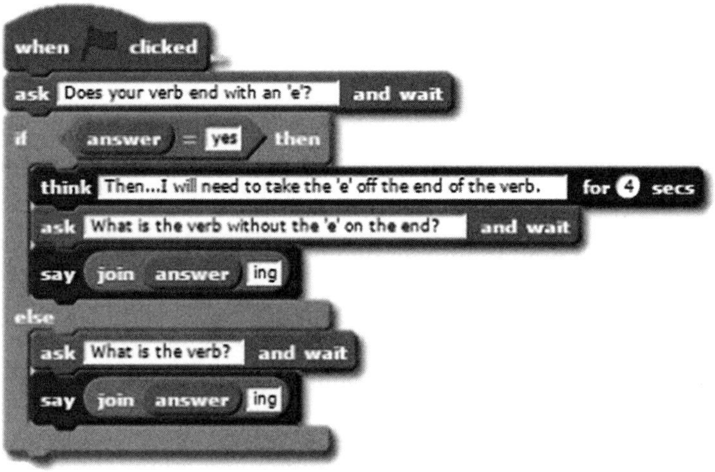

Figure 4.2. Algorithm used in the *No Fear Coding* lesson on the present participle.

The full lesson plan includes three differentiated versions for educator use. If you see an asterisk in the front of the project name, this means that the lesson has been STRETCh'ed to support ESL and struggling learners. If you see an asterisk after the project name, this means that the lesson has been STRETCh'ed to support advanced learners. You can download the full lesson from the *No Fear Coding* website (**Nofearcoding.org**).

While the lesson above uses Scratch, an educator could use any of the visual block programming languages. The focus of this lesson incorporates the Common Core State Standards in English language arts, specifically in the strand of conventions of standard English (L.1.2.D), which states "Use conventional spelling for words with common spelling patterns and for frequently occurring irregular words."

While the standard covered does not lend itself to the abilities of most first-grade students, it is an excellent lesson for gifted first grade students. Second grade students could also use a lesson such as this to review the first-grade ELA standard and apply their knowledge of computational thinking in the areas of algorithms and procedures and data analysis.

Computational Thinking in Action

To better understand how to apply computational thinking skills, let's break apart the steps needed to conduct a Kindergarten author study (simulation). For an author study, teachers introduce students to a famous author and the potential books they will be reading. To set the purpose, the teacher lets the students know they will be exploring the following essential question: What are our opinions of Eric Carle's books?

As a class, time should then be spent breaking down the essential question (problem decomposition) by asking some further questions such as: How will we record our opinions? What kind of opinions will we collect? How many opinions will we collect? Why are we collecting our opinions? What will we do with our opinions? This process of problem decomposition is important to model for students, as it is a necessary step in student understanding of how to research.

Next, the answers to the questions during problem decomposition become the algorithms and procedures that will be used throughout the simulation. For the purpose of this example, students have decided that they will be recording their opinions on how well the pictures help them visualize the written story. The class has also determined that 24 opinions for each book would be too many to analyze (go through), so they have decided to break into groups and each book will have four opinions. Once they reached this point, a student asked: How many pictures per book will we need? The class decided on four pictures per book.

Thus, there will be six groups of four students each. Each group will study one Eric Carle book. The teacher has also helped students to create the following sentence frame (a form of automation) to record their opinions:

I think the picture _____ helps me to visualize the story because _____.

Students will be required to write "does" or "does not" in the first blank of each frame, followed by their opinion. Teachers provide support as needed.

Next on the agenda is to determine what students will do with their opinions. The class elicits ideas and it is determined that this might be good information for the author to receive, similar to when the teacher tells them how they can improve their work. They decide that their opinions will be published and shared with their parents and Eric Carle via a blog. Concerned students point out that they don't know how to spell all the words they have in their head, and the teacher assures them they will revise their work so that it has correct spelling when they send the published product to the author.

As a class, they then write down their procedures for their author study so they can engage in their data collection.

Step 1: Teacher reads the books to the class.

Step 2: Students look at their assigned book and determine if the pictures help them visualize the words.

Step 3: Students draft their opinions, using the sentence frame and providing a reason for their thinking.

Step 4: Students review and revise their work. (During this step teachers will meet with small groups and begin collecting commonly used words and ideas from their opinion writing (data analysis). A word wall (automation) will be created to help support student spelling, as well as a class graphic organizer that contains main ideas (abstraction) of their thinking.

Step 5: Students will publish their opinions (data representation).

Step 6: Published work will be shared with parents and Eric Carle via a blog page (parallelization).

By having teachers think through the project with the lens of computational thinking, it will provide students with the skill set they need to be lifelong 21st century learners. This process can be replicated with any number of content areas. You will see a variety of examples embedded throughout this book.

Case Study: Gardening Programs in the Elementary School

Karen North, retired technology teacher from Houston Independent School District and current computer science education consultant, sponsored a Computer Science STEM Green Club at Piney Point Elementary School in Houston to integrate coding and environmental education. The motto of the club was "Taking care of our brains so we can take care of the Earth" and the focus was on Next Generation Science Standard 2-LS2-1, which states: "Plan and conduct an investigation to determine if plants need sunlight and water to grow."

The learning experience started when Karen, along with 50 volunteers, read the book *Farmer Will Allen and the Growing Table*, to a class of second graders. Students were then asked what seeds they would like to plant. After deciding upon marigold seeds, students learned about algorithms and how they help people do everyday activities by the "Real-life Algorithms: Planting a Seed" video (**youtu.be/FHsuEh1kJ18**) from the Code.org Course 1 lesson on algorithms (**code.org/curriculum/course1/6/teacher**). This 20-minute lesson is a great way to engage students in algorithmic thinking while relating the steps involved in everyday activities. It uses the process of planting a seed but the exercise can be done with any activity or event you are teaching.

Piney Point students were given the Code.org lesson worksheet for the lesson (an "unplugged" lesson that doesn't require a computer). The worksheet displays the steps involved in planting a seed (along with some incorrect steps that students must identify) in picture squares that students cut out and arrange in the correct sequence. Collaborating in groups, students engaged with the components of critical thinking by communicating with each other to problem solve the steps needed and the order in which they are performed. To test their procedures, students needed to run through the steps in order from beginning to end to make sure they made sense (computing the process).

Students then planted marigold seeds following the steps from the algorithm. While they were growing, students explored flower patterns and the Common Core Math Standard **2.GA.1**, which states, "Recognize and draw shapes having specified attributes, such as a given number of angles or a given number of equal faces." There are a number of ways to practice this standard using coding. For this class, students practiced making fractals with the Code.org lesson Code with Anna and Elsa (**studio.code.org/s/frozen/stage/1/puzzle/1**). They also coded digital flowers using Scratch and sent them as virtual cards to relatives by sharing the link to their projects.

Code.org has a K-5 Curriculum Course guide that outlines standards covered in each of the lessons. Table 4.1 outlines the standards covered in the above second grade case study.

TABLE 4.1. Standards addressed in Code.org lesson "Real-life Algorithms–Plant a Seed

REAL-LIFE ALGORITHMS – PLANT A SEED (UNPLUGGED)	
ISTE Standards for Students	**1.a:** Apply existing knowledge to generate new ideas, products, or processes. **4.b:** Plan and manage activities to develop a solution or complete a project.
Next Generation Science Standards	**2-LS2-1:** Plan and conduct an investigation to determine if plants need sunlight and water to grow.
Common Core Math Standards and Practices	**Math.Content.2.GA.1:** Recognize and draw shapes having specified attributes, such as a given number of angles or a given number of equal faces. **Mathematical Practice 3**: Construct viable arguments and critique the reasoning of others.
Common Core English Language Arts Standards	**ELA-Literacy.SL.2.1:** Participate in collaborative conversations with diverse partners about grade 2 topics and texts with peers and adults in small and larger groups. **ELA-Literacy.SL2.2:** Recount or describe key ideas or details from a text read aloud or information presented orally or through other media.

Case Study: Binary Bracelets

First grade students from Piney Point Elementary School in Houston took part in a special computational thinking exercise on October 10, 2011, or Binary Day (10-1-11). Students completed the Code.org activity Binary Bracelets and were given an assessment in which a message was written with binary numbers. Their final assessment was graded on their ability to decode the message.

The full video of a Piney Point Elementary student working through the project can be found on the **Nofearcoding.org** website. In the words of one expert:

"I put 'L' here...but then I thought that wasn't right and I put 'J' there...but I didn't think that was right and I thought to myself maybe I should follow these...so I didn't understand what to do. Then I just looked for the 'C' and the 'E,' and the 'U," and I figured out just now that it just said, 'Coding is fun.' I'm going to be a computer scientist."

Can you figure out what the message says?

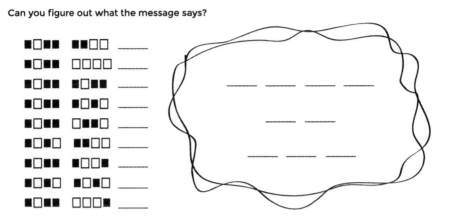

Figure 4.3. Binary Bracelet activity worksheet.

The full lesson can be found at **code.org/curriculum/unplugged**. The standards addressed in the lesson are shown in Table 4.2.

TABLE 4.2. Standards addressed in Code.org lesson "Binary Bracelets"

BINARY BRACELETS (UNPLUGGED)	
ISTE Standards	**1.c:** Use models and simulation to explore complex systems and issues. **6.a:** Understand and use technology systems.
Next-Generation Science Standards	**K–2-PS3-2:** Use tools and materials provided to design and build a device that solves a specific problem or a solution to a specific problem. **K–2-ETS1-1:** Ask questions, make observations, and gather information about a situation people want to change to define a simple problem that can be solved through the development of a new or improved object or tool.
Common Core Math Practices	**Mathematical Practice 7:** Look for and make use of structure.

Computational Thinking Lesson Plans

Google Computational Thinking Lesson Plans

Google has a variety of lesson plans that have been aligned to Common Core State Standards (CCSS) in math and literacy, as well as Next Generation Science Standards (NGSS), ISTE Standards, and CSTA standards.

Ciphering a Sentence (suggested ages: 8–12): This lesson plan enables students to develop a cipher, encode a sentence, and then develop an algorithm for encoding and decoding.

Describing an Everyday Object (suggested ages: 8–15): This lesson plan explores the difficulty of providing detailed descriptions of objects without using their names. The computational thinking concepts covered include abstraction, data representation, and pattern recognition.

Exploring Your Environment (suggested ages: 8–12): This lesson plan enables students to gather data about a place or environment, organize that data in a table, and look for patterns. The computational thinking concepts covered include data collection, data representation, data analysis, and decomposition.

Solving a Guessing Game with Data (suggested ages: 8–12): This lesson plan requires students to develop two guessing games. The computational thinking concepts covered include data collection, data representation, data analysis, and algorithm design.

Mystery Word X (suggested ages: 8–10): This lesson plan enables students to analyze the classification of nouns and verbs. They begin by considering nouns as "a person, place or thing" and verbs as "action" words. They then run a group of words through a series of "tests" and identify instances in which this standard notion might lead to errors.

To see all lesson plans visit **goo.gl/4Pnww6**.

Lemonade Stand

The premise of this lesson is a simulation where the task is to plan, supply, and run a lemonade stand with the goal of making as much money possible in 14 days. The lesson takes a popular math game and extends it to teach computational thinking concepts (shown in Table 4.3). A full set of lesson plans for this activity can be found at **Nofearcoding.org**.

TABLE 4.3. Lemonade Stand lesson activities aligned to computational thinking concepts.

CT CONCEPT AND DEFINITION	TASK
SIMULATION **Representation of model of a process. Simulation also involves running experiments using models**	In 14 days, make as much money as you can from a virtual lemonade stand. Create a presentation for Bank Q that will support either closing or expanding your lemonade stand.
PROBLEM DECOMPOSITION **Breaking down tasks into smaller manageable parts**	Create a list of steps needed to prepare for your presentation. Purchase supplies. Sell lemonade.
ALGORITHMS AND PROCEDURES **Series of ordered steps taken to solve a problem or achieve some end**	Analyze temperature and weather forecast, purchase supplies, set prices, sell lemonade, re-evaluate, and repeat.
DATA COLLECTION **The process of gathering appropriate information**	Track supplies, purchased sales, potential customers, customer satisfaction, popularity and profit/loss each day on a spreadsheet.
AUTOMATION **Having computers or machines do repetitive or tedious tasks**	Play Cool Math Lemonade Stand game **(coolmath-games.com/0-lemonade-stand)**. Use Google Sheets or Excel to track data.
DATA ANALYSIS **Making sense of data, finding patterns, and drawing conclusions**	Analyze data on spreadsheet to draw conclusions to support closing or expanding the business.
ABSTRACTION **Reducing complexity to define main idea**	Make as much profit as possible.
DATA REPRESENTATION **Depicting and organizing data in appropriate graphs, charts, words or images**	Create graphs and charts to support your presentation to Bank Q.
PARALLELIZATION **Organize resources to simultaneously carry out tasks to reach a common goal**	Put together a presentation for the executive board of Bank Q in support of closing or expanding your lemonade stand business based on gathered data.

PART 2

Engaging Young Coders with Bee-Bots

Younger learners benefit from hands-on, concrete representations of concepts. Part two looks at how coding and computational thinking skills can be fostered through the use of the programmable robot Bee-Bot. In this section you will learn:

- How Bee-Bots work and why to use them
- What teaching with Bee-Bots looks like
- Lessons and case studies using Bee-Bots across the curriculum

CHAPTER 5

Why Teach with Bee-Bots?

The Bee-Bot is one of the best tools available to start a learner on the road to mastering computational and critical thinking skills. This bee shaped, programmable robot makes the essential skill of decision making easy with just four movement commands and three control commands. Reducing the complexity of a problem builds the process of learning how to solve problems and increases students' automaticity (fluency). In addition to problem solving, Bee-Bots also serve as an excellent introduction to the computer science practices of creativity, collaboration, communication, persistence, and problem solving.

Since Bee-Bots are usually used with groups of two to four students, they also present opportunities for students to work on the Common Core State Standards in English Language Arts, specifically in the areas of speaking and listening.

Figure 5.1. Students using Bee-Bot to spell words.

There are also many opportunities for social learning when working with Bee-Bots, such as lessons in sharing.

Developmental Progression of Skills

Elementary teachers understand the importance of using manipulatives with their younger learners. Most students progress through the learning of a concept by beginning with the concrete before moving to the representational and, finally, the abstract. Figure 5.2 shows an example of concrete, representational, and abstract ways of representing the number three; with physical objects, symbolic marks in place of physical objects, and finally with an abstract numeral. Bee-Bots are an ideal concrete resource for introducing coding to younger learners using the Concrete-Representational-Abstract (CRA) instructional approach. Once students have mastered the concrete stage of physically programming an object to make it move they can continue their learning with cardinal directions in the representational stage using a resource such as Code.org Course 1. Students can then move to the abstract by using Scratch to learn how to manipulate code blocks in order to make the characters, or "sprites" as they are referred to in Scratch, move and act.

Figure 5.2. Concrete, representational, and abstract depictions of the number 3.

Another reason for K–5 teachers to use Bee-Bots in their classrooms is the number of literacy and math connections that can be made within the concrete level of learning. For example, in order for the Bee-Bot to move from one location to another, the correct sequence must be input by the user. It also exposes young students to the written language of code. The use of these highly engaging robots also supports the skills of counting, problem solving, and cause and effect, as well as supporting concepts of print with left-to-right reading.

The best way to learn how to integrate the Bee-Bot is hands-on, sitting on the floor watching the kids play and asking questions. Connect these questions to current curriculum concepts. Just imagine the traditional weather calendar moving from the wall or the interactive whiteboard to the floor, with students programming a Bee-Bot to move from the start to the hot weather symbol, or to the correct day of the week.

Developing Identify

Supporting social learning and providing roles for group members when programming the Bee-Bots helps young coders develop self-identities that they can become engineers and coders. When working with groups of four, the following roles can be used:

The programmer lays out the programming cards in the correct order.

The input engineer presses the correct buttons on the Bee-Bot to input the program from the cards.

The debugger watches the Bee-Bot for errors and reports them.

The recorder receives the debugger's report and notes the arrow cards that did not run correctly.

One of the most important reasons why K–5 educators will want to incorporate Bee-Bots into their instruction is student engagement. The best lessons are those the students create, with the teacher providing the questions and a few examples.

Allowing Depth of Knowledge to Flow Naturally

Another reason why Bee-Bots can be useful to the classroom teacher is that one can easily incorporate all four levels of Norman Webb's Depth of Knowledge (DOK) Levels. For those of us who have been around a bit longer, we are more familiar with Bloom's Taxonomy.

The biggest difference between the two models is that within Bloom's Taxonomy, the idea is to move from one level to the next and includes the ability to pick from and stay on a level. With DOK, the idea is that learning needs the following levels working together:

Level 1: Recall. Recall a fact, information, or procedure. Process information on a low level.

Level 2: Skill/ Concept. Use information or conceptual knowledge, two or more steps

Level 3: Strategic Thinking. Requires reasoning, developing a plan or a sequence of steps.

Level 4: Extended Thinking. Requires an investigation, time to think and process multiple conditions of the problem.

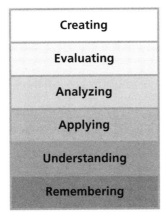

Bloom's Taxonomy

Creating
Evaluating
Analyzing
Applying
Understanding
Remembering

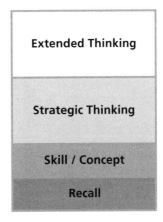

Webb's Depth of Knowledge

Extended Thinking
Strategic Thinking
Skill / Concept
Recall

Figure 5.3. Levels of thinking in Bloom's Taxonomy and Webb's Depth of Knowledge.

For this reason, DOK is a better fit for computational thinking and computer science. In the world of computer science, depth of knowledge when using Bee-Bots can be seen outlined in Table 5.1.

TABLE 5.1. Depth of knowledge and application to Bee-Bots

DOK LEVEL	DEFINITION WITHIN COMPUTER SCIENCE	APPLICATION TO BEE-BOTS
LEVEL 1 **Recall and Reproduction**	The recall of definitions, terms or simple procedures in which the student knows the answer or does not.	Knowing what a Bee-Bot is Turning the Bee-Bot on and off Pushing the arrow buttons Understanding the up arrow moves forward, the down arrow moves back, the right arrow moves right and the left arrow moves left
LEVEL 2 **Skill / Concept**	The process of making decisions on how to approach a question or problem.	What were you trying to get your robot to do? What do you think the Bee-Bot will do if you put in these commands?

Table continues on following page.

DOK LEVEL	DEFINITION WITHIN COMPUTER SCIENCE	APPLICATION TO BEE-BOTS
LEVEL 3 **Strategic Thinking**	Requires reasoning, planning, using evidence, and is a multi-step process. Often there are multiple answers or multiple ways to arrive at the answer.	How did you get the Bee-Bot to do that? Why do we need rules? Why didn't the Bee-Bot do what you wanted it to do?
LEVEL 4 **Extended Thinking**	Requires students to make several connections within a content area or among content areas. Involves developing generalizations of the results obtained, the strategies used, and then applying these to a new situation.	How can you build on ideas you see and collaborate on new ones? Can you create your own game with the Bee-Bot?

CHAPTER 6

How to Teach with Bee-Bots

What makes Bee-Bots appealing to young students also makes them fun to use in the classroom. Students are motivated, active, and ready to engage with computational thinking concepts. By introducing students to this kind of entry level programming, you may be opening the door for a continued interest in robotics and coding. This chapter presents approaches to teaching with Bee-Bots and advice on acquiring materials—including how to teach Bee-Bot skills and concepts without a Bee-Bot. The chapter features six activities designed to get students (and teachers) familiar with using Bee-Bots and progress through all of the commands needed to be able to create your own Bee-Bot activities to fit within your curriculum.

Instructional Approaches for Using Bee-Bots

When using Bee-Bots, it is useful to have questions ready to guide inquiry. The questions shared below incorporate Webb's Depth of Knowledge (DOK) levels discussed in the previous chapter. Often, administrators are looking to come in and observe a lesson that incorporates the use of DOK questions in action. What a better way to get administrators passionate about the use of coding within the curriculum you are already teaching.

Bee-Bot Prompting Questions

- How did you get the Bee-Bot to do that?

- What were you trying to get the Bee-Bot to do?

- Why didn't the Bee-Bot do what you wanted it to?

- What do you think the Bee-Bot will do if you put in these commands … ?

- Can you write a sequence of steps and guess where the Bee-Bot will go?

- Can you teach the Bee-Bot to add 3 + 4? Or to go to a letter in your name?

- Why do we need rules?

- How can you build on ideas you see and collaborate on new ones?

- Can you create your own game with the Bee-Bot?

Design Thinking

When working with Bee-Bots, it is helpful to look at the design thinking process (Figure 5.1). This process is cyclical and there is a lot of back and forth between the stages, especially for our youngest coders. The stages of the design thinking process are: empathy, definition, ideation, prototype, and testing (Figure 6.1).

Empathy involves creating a "user centered" solution.

Definition requires interpreting what you learned to identify what the user needs.

Ideation is the process of generating, advancing, and communicating ideas.

Prototyping allows for manipulation and testing of ideas using a prototype or preliminary copy.

Testing involves refining the prototype based on user feedback.

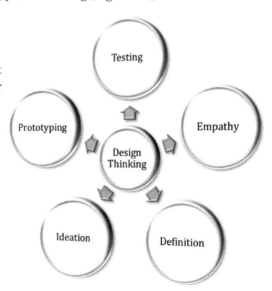

Figure 6.1. Design thinking process.

You will see these stages reflected in the Bee-Bot activities within this chapter. Keep in mind that this process considers the social and emotional components of computer science. There are many opportunities to help our students feel compassion and empathy for the problems that others face. These are characteristics that will help build ethical and strong future leaders.

Bee-Bot Learning Materials

The activities in this chapter are designed for one Bee-Bot or ideally a 6-pack or "Hive" of Bee-Bots (Figure 6.2) If you don't have access to a Bee-Bot, you can also do these activities using just the directional arrow cards, which can be downloaded for free at **Nofearcoding.org**. Another alternative is to use students as "real-life" Bee-Bots by having them stand and follow commands given their classmates. This can be almost as engaging for students as using the robots themselves and is a great option for teachers who do not have access to Bee-Bots.

Figure 6.2. Bee-Bot Hive set.

WHERE TO GET BEE-BOTS

Bee Bots can be purchased, along with lesson mats and accessories, direct from the Terrapin website (**www.bee-bot.us**). Terrapin published the Logo computer language and related instructional materials, including Logo "turtle robots" that provide a hands-on expression of the Logo philosophy. Bee-Bot, Blue-Bot, and Pro-Bot are the latest versions of these robots.

GRANTS AND FUNDING

Spring Branch ISD in Houston, Texas wrote a grant to purchase a Bee-Bot learning set for every elementary school in their district. With the focus on technology and STEM projects, there are many opportunities for grants. Start by checking with your district or with your Parent Teacher Association or Parent Teacher Organization to see if they could help provide funds as well.

Bee-Bot Lesson Mats

Bee-Bot lesson mats are the surface that Bee-Bots move across. They can be blank grids or feature numers and letters. Lesson mats can be purchased or you can create your own. To get ideas or save time there are a variety of resources available online. For example, Della Larsen's Teachers-Pay-Teachers store (**teacherspay-teachers.com/Store/Della-Larsens-Class**) is full of Bee-Bot activities. She has a math Tangram activity, a science frog life cycle activity, and many others.

The website for this book (**Nofearcoding.org**) has a variety of Bee-Bot lesson mats that can be downloaded and printed for use with science, social studies, math, and literacy lessons. Free resources can also be found at **www.tes.com/us** by simply putting "Bee-Bots" in the search bar. There are instruction cards and a variety of Bee-Bot mats that can be printed for different content areas.

Bee-Bot Activities

The activities in this chapter are designed to get students comfortable with using Bee-Bots, beginning with the simple goals of play and movement. The lessons advance to more complicated movement control and a challenge. The activities can be done using one or more Bee-Bots, using only the arrow cards (download them at **Nofearcoding.org**), or using arrow cards and student stand-ins.

Lesson Format

The learning activities presented in this section follow the same computational thinking process:

Input > Process > Output > Feedback

Beginning with a goal, students determine which commands to input. The Bee-Bot processes and follows these commands. Students observe the output (what happens as a result of the Bee-Bot processing the commands) and share feedback. The cycle may be repeated as needed to reach the desired goal.

Activity 1: Have Fun

"Not all the paths we take get us to a destination." The goal of this introductory lesson is to have fun and get comfortable with the Bee-Bot.

Materials

- One or more Bee-Bots (or arrow cards to be used with students in place of Bee-Bots)
- Lesson mat with grid

Rules

1. Students sit around the lesson mat.
2. Tell students to not touch the control commands (Clear, Pause, or Go). They should only touch the orange arrow commands."

Input directional commands in turn

1. Hand a Bee-Bot to a student who inputs a directional command.
2. Pass to the student on right who inputs another directional command.
3. Continue going around in a circle and stop after all students have added a command, or after a certain amount of time has passed.

Process the Bee-Bot commands

1. Put Bee-Bot(s) on a square on the mat.
2. Select a student to input the Go button.

Output observation: Watch what the Bee-Bot(s) does

1. Watch and observe. Did the Bee-Bot go off the mat?
2. When using more than one Bee-Bot, did they bump into each other?

Feedback: Discuss what happened

1. Discuss what rules could prevent going off the mat or bumping into each other.
2. Allow students to play again and observe them making plans.
3. Let students play as long as they are engaged and settle their own arguments.
4. Should you have to intervene, ask these questions:
   a. What did you do? If the student starts talking about the other students, repeat, "what were *you* doing?"
   b. What could you have done differently? What else could you have done?

Assessment

1. Switch groups and have students pass around the Bee-Bots.
2. Ask them what will happen when the Go button is selected.

Activity 2: **Moving Forward**

In this activity, students use pair programming to master the forward command by moving the Bee-Bot to a specified location. Pair programming is a computer science technique where two programmers work together at one station or computer so that one can write code while the other reviews it, switching roles as needed. You may want to explain the term and show the code.org video that explains pair programming for elementary students (**studio.code.org/s/course1/stage/3/puzzle/1**) before beginning the activity.

Materials

- One or more Bee-Bots (or arrow cards to be used with students in place of Bee-Bots)
- Lesson mat

Rules

1. Students work in pairs. The students on the edges of the mat are the drivers who enter commands into the Bee-Bot. The students on the corners of the mat are the navigators who review the commands and how the Bee-Bot moves.

2. Use only the Forward, Clear, and Go commands.

3. The Bee-bot is placed on a square on the edge and parallel to the lines on the mat.

Input forward commands to go to a specified letter.

1. Have a navigator pick a square on the lesson mat.

2. The driver writes or says the sequence of steps (algorithm) needed to get to the square.

3. The driver will input the forward commands to get to the square.

Process the Bee-Bot commands

1. Place the robot where it will go in a straight line to the specified square.

2. Students can practice this by walking in a straight line and counting their steps.

3. The driver pushes the Go command.

Output observation: Watch what the Bee-Bot(s) does

1. Observe. Did the Bee-Bot go to the correct letter?
2. When using more than one Bee-Bot, did they bump into each other?

Feedback

Facilitate discussion by asking the following types of questions.

1. How many forward commands did you input?
2. If the Bee-Bot did not go to the correct letter, how did you debug the problem?
3. Can you play until everyone gets a chance to go to their favorite letters? Trade places between being the navigator and driver.
4. Were any letters left out?

Assessment

See if every student in the group has mastered using the forward command by asking them to go to a square of their choice. Students can check each other.

Note: It is essential to master this small step before adding more commands. Just like in solving math problems, you need to master understanding addition before starting subtraction.

Activity 3: **Moving to a Location**

The goal of this activity is to master control of the left and right turn arrows by moving the Bee-Bot to a specified location. It incorporates the same pair programming technique used in Activity 2.

Materials

- One or more Bee-Bots (or arrow cards to be used with students in place of Bee-Bots)
- Lesson mat with letters of the alphabet

Rules

The Process is the same as in Activity 2. But this time the Bee-Bot will be placed where the students must turn right or left to get to the letter. Standing up and physically moving like the Bee-Bot helps the students master this added challenge.

Assessment

Ask students to spell a one-letter word. Place the Bee-Bot on the letter "Z." Watch to see if students go to letters other than "A" or "I."

 (Literacy) ## Activity 4: **Spelling**

The goal of this lesson is to control movement of the Bee-Bot and to use the backward command.

Rules

The Process is the same as in Activity Two, but this time the Pause command will be selected when the desired letter is reached. The Backward command should be used to efficiently move to another letter. Some students may turn around instead of backing up. Work with these students on spatial reasoning skills. In the previous activity, students walked out their plans. This time have them plan on paper by writing out the "code" using arrows to show how they would get to the letter. To check the code, have students program the Bee-Bot and push the Go command.

Assessment

Have students spell a CVC (consonant-vowel-consonant) word they should have mastered in spelling lessons, such as "red" or "bat." Have teams write a sentence using CVC words and give to another group. Each team member codes one of the words.

Activity 5: **Line Dancing with the Bees**

In this activity, students will practice movement commands and program the Bee-Bot to do a line dance. In preparation, have students watch the Dancing with the Bees Video, which shows students from Piney Point Elementary School's Girl Tech Club performing the dance with Bee-Bots (**cscurriculum.shutterfly.com/35**).

Rules

1. Movement must be in a line

2. Keep dance simple, no more than 10 steps

3. Loop the dance steps

Input

Share the following dance steps with students by acting them out.

1. Move forward three steps.

2. Turn right, wiggle like a bee, turn left, turn left, wiggle like a bee, turn right.

3. Move backward three steps.

4. Repeat second bullet.

5. Repeat the whole process one or two more times.

6. Free dance like a bee.

Process

1. Students write down the sequence of steps for this line dance.

2. Students code the Bee-Bot to follow their directions.

3. Determine which steps in the line dance the Bee-Bot can't do?

Output

1. Put the Bee-Bot on the mat and see if it can do the dance.

2. If using more than one Bee-Bot, try to synchronize the robots.

3. Try to do the dance with the Bee-Bots.

Feedback

Facilitate discussion by asking the following types of questions.

1. Were you successful?

2. Could you design your own line dance?

3. Did each dancer stay in a line?

4. Can you make up new rules that allow moving off the line?

Assessment

Ask the students to perform the steps in the dance with the Bee-Bots.

Literacy Activity 6: **Spelling Bee**

This activity challenges students to use all the Bee-Bot commands while performing a robotic spelling bee.

Rules

1. All commands must be programmed before placing the Bee-Bot on the mat and selecting the Go command.

2. The Bee-Bot starts in the top left-hand corner at the letter "A," facing downward toward the bottom left corner.

3. Students are spelling the words in the sentence: "I want to design a present for my brain."

4. In the first round, students start with the one-letter word "I" and program the Bee-Bot to move to it and then pause before moving to the next word.

5. In the second round, students program the Bee-Bot to spell a two-letter word from the sentence. Subsequent rounds have Bee-Bot spelling 3-letter and 4-letter words, continuing until the 7-letter word is programmed.

Input

1. Watch a video of a student performing a robotic spelling bee: **cscurriculum. shutterfly.com/48**

2. Select student teams of two to four students.

3. Inform students that there is no talking when coding.

Process

1. Each team codes a word.

2. When not the driver, the other members of the team are observers.

3. There is no help given while the commands are coded.

Output

1. The Bee-bot moves on the mat, pausing on each letter in the word.

2. If the word is spelled correctly, the team advances to next level.

Feedback

1. If there is an error, the team helps the student debug their mistake and tries again.

2. The class determines how many tries each person gets before being eliminated on each level.

3. Discuss efficiency and how many commands the Bee-Bot can remember.

Assessment

Make up a new sentence and have the students coordinate a new spelling bee challenge.

CHAPTER

7

Bee-Bots in the Classroom— Case Studies

Teachers looking to incorporate Bee-Bots can benefit from reading accounts of their use in the classroom. This chapter includes case studies from elementary teachers who have successfully used Bee-Bots to teach literacy and math concepts. You can read other accounts of teachers' experiences with Bee-Bots on the Terrapin website (**bee-bot.us**) under "Stories."

Bee-Bots and Basic Math

Kathy Cassidy holds professional development sessions for teachers about using technology in their classrooms, including the use of robots. Kathy also teaches first grade at Westmount School in Moose Jaw, Canada.

Students in Kathy's classroom recently began to use Bee-Bots as an entry into programing and coding. To learn about how Bee-Bots work and the variety of commands available, they worked in groups to lay out a sequence of actions to get the Bee-Bot to travel to a specific square. Kathy said that through this hands-on process the children could see different groups choosing different routes to get to the same place. She says that "there was lots of trial and error learning and eventually the students discovered that there were many ways to accomplish the same task."

Figure 7.1. First-grade students using Bee-Bot for addition
and subtraction. Source: Kathy Cassidy

Kathy became very creative with her use of Bee-Bots in the classroom. She describes
how she and the Bee-Bot helped students who were struggling to understand the
concept of one and two more and less than a number.

> I used floor tape to make a twenty-space, one-column grid and had the
> students put the numbers from one to twenty in their places on a number
> line. The students and I then talked about the concepts of more and less
> with the Bee-Bot. Which way would the Bee-Bot go on the number line if a
> number was more? Less? The forward and backward arrows on the Bee-Bot
> were an effective visual representation of this. Before we programmed the
> Bee-Bot to move, I placed the Bee-Bot somewhere on the number line grid
> and posed questions such as "Where will the Bee-Bot stop on the number
> line if the number was two more?" or "What if the Bee-Bot moves to one less
> than this number? Where will it stop?" I had the students write their names
> on a sticky note and predict where the Bee-Bot would be at the end of the
> program. Once everyone had made their prediction, one of the students
> programmed the Bee-Bot to move the specified number of spaces and we
> watched to see who had made the correct predictions. Students had some
> difficulty on the first couple of attempts, but soon all the students were able
> to accurately predict what one or two more or less would be. Success using
> the Bee-Bot for this practical and fun visual representation!

Kathy documents her students' progress with Bee-Bots and other classroom activities on her blog (**mscassidysclass.edublogs.org**).

Alpha-Robotics

Bee-Bots are being piloted with pre-kindergartners, kindergartners, first-, and second-graders in seven Boston Public Schools as part of a K–12 Engineering Pathway Grant initiated by TechBoston, the district-wide office that oversees technology integration in the schools.

Leading the Bee-Bot introductions is Judy Robinson Fried, STEM curriculum consultant for Alpha-Robotics (**alpharobotics.com**), a resource for elementary teachers using a multi-disciplinary approach to teach engineering concepts using robots. Judy has led both teacher training workshops and in-class presentations on using Bee-Bots in the classroom. She finds that both students and teachers are excited about use of Bee-Bots and quickly learn to program them.

As part of introducing Bee-Bots, Alpha-Robotics has developed customized materials for use in Boston Public School classrooms. These include special mats, programming blocks, and image cards. These materials allow use of Bee-Bots in many different areas and channel the motivation Bee-Bots inspire to teach a variety of subjects, from mathematics to language arts.

Students in Boston Public Schools are ethnically and culturally diverse and Bee-Bots have proven highly effective for cutting through language and cultural barriers. Judy was especially enthusiastic about her experience with the students and teachers in a K1 and K2 Vietnamese sheltered English class. She reports, "the students have done a spectacular job of programming the Bee-Bot to travel on different paths on any mat. I would say about 80% have created complicated programs. (Fried, n.d.)."

Community in Schools

Akin Elementary School in Hale Center, Texas is conducting a summer learning program through a "Community in Schools" grant provided by Ace 21st Century. Interested students in grades 1 through 8 filled all the classes through advance registration. Science classes feature introductory robotics using Bee-Bot and Pro-Bot (Bee-Bot's "older brother"). Course teacher Lester Carr used challenges from his book *Problem Solving with Bee-Bot* to introduce robotics to younger students.

Excitement ran high as students were introduced to Bee-Bots and practiced using the controls. Though none of the students had previous experience using Bee-Bots, students in grades 1 through 3 were soon able to move Bee-Bots to various locations on their grid mats. After learning the basics, students worked in pairs to solve challenges at higher levels of difficulty.

Fourth grade students start with harder problems from *Problem Solving with Bee-Bot*. After some head scratching and comments like "I didn't tell it to go there, did I?" or "Why did it go *there*?" success is enjoyed by all with high-fives. Students work 30 of the more than 150 problems in the book and then may create their own or work other "special" problems.

Students in grades 5 through 8 use Pro-Bot to solve challenging problems with the Pro-Bot Route Mat. This involves calculating various angles and even developing circular paths as they navigate routes on the mat. This helps students to develop geometry skills in reading angles as well as decision-making skills in selecting alternate routes to arrive at their destination.

A very popular part of the course is using Pro-Bot's capability to carry a pen to draw pictures and shapes. Using Pro-Bot's pen up-down feature, students develop procedures on the robot with which they draw different geometric patterns and other designs. Learn more about Pro-Bot at **bee-bot.us/probot.html**.

PART

3

Introduce Coding with Code.org

Thanks to Code.org, access to coding tutorials and opportunities to practice computational thinking skills is readily available and incredibly easy to incorporate across the curriculum. This section explores some of the available resources Code.org offers for K–5 educators. You will learn:

- How Code.org and its mission is changing the world
- Which Code.org activities are appropriate for different content areas
- What teaching with Code.org looks like

CHAPTER

8

Why Introduce Students to Coding with Code.org?

Code.org was founded in 2013 with the primary mission of promoting computer science. The organization believes that every student in every school should have the opportunity to learn computer science. While this is a great concept in theory, it is much more difficult for the K–5 teacher to fit into their already full schedule. However, it is essential that we find ways to do so. According to Code.org,

> Computing is a fundamental part of daily life, commerce, and just about every occupation in our modern economy. It is essential that students are exposed to the field of computer science in our K–12 system—as it is foundational in transforming the way a student thinks about the world. It not only teaches them about technology, it also teaches them how to think differently about any problem. Computer science puts students on the path toward some of the highest paying, fastest growing jobs in America. (Code.org, 2017)

As of this publication, Code.org states that only 40% of our schools teach computer programming to students. More shocking is that only 8% of students graduating from STEM (Science, Technology, Engineering, and Mathematics) programs go into the field of computer science; however, 71% of all new jobs in STEM are in computing (Code.org, 2017). Thus, exposing all students to computer science, beginning in kindergarten, is essential.

Diversity within Computer Science Careers

With only 20% of girls entering high school computer science, the diversity problem begins in K–12. The good news is that women who try AP Computer science in high school are ten times more likely to major in it in college. The statistics for African American and Hispanic students show that they are seven times more likely to major in computer science in college if exposed to it during their K–12 educational career.

Each year, the Code.org website updates its data on diversity by surveying the students who have active accounts under the guidance of teachers. Their data currently shows that 48% of these students come from traditionally underrepresented minorities. This would include Black, Hispanic, Pacific Islander, and Native American students. Forty-eight percent of the students actively using Code.org come from economically disadvantaged homes where students receive free or reduced meal programs. While this data is merely representational, as Code.org protects the privacy by making their survey optional, it still shows that they are making a difference in reaching students of underrepresented ethnic groups.

Code.org Is Making a Difference

If you desire to be an early adopter and you are not a follower of the Code.org blog, "Anybody Can Learn," you may want to sign up now. Code.org researchers have been studying the impact of the Hour of Code on attitudes toward self-efficacy with computer science. The resources complied for the Hour of Code and for use beyond this event hope to expose students to engaging curriculum and learning experiences that change misconceptions some may have about the field of computer science.

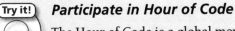

Try it! *Participate in Hour of Code*

The Hour of Code is a global movement reaching tens of millions of students in more than 180 countries. No experience is necessary and anyone can organize an Hour of Code event. For tutorials and more information visit **hourofcode.com**.

The research done immediately before and after the Hour of Code was based on a 4-point likert scale that used the following statements:

- I like computer science

- I think computer science is interesting.

- I have the ability to learn computer science.

- I am better at computer science than most kids at my school.

It should be noted that the first two statements comprise the construct of "attitude" in the studies, while the second two comprise the construct of "self-efficacy." The pre-survey also included a question on previous experience, allowing students one of three options: never done an Hour of Code, only done an Hour of Code, done more than an Hour of Code.

The findings of the study concluded that there were statistically significant changes in students attitudes toward and self-efficacy with computer science after engaging in just one Hour of Code activity. Most students in the study engaged in only 40 minutes of tutorials, but this suggests that simple exposure to computer science might be a critical first step in engaging underrepresented groups, especially females, in the area of computer science (Phillips & Brooks, 2017).

CHAPTER 9

How to Use Code.org within the Curriculum

U sing Code.org is easy and free. All you need to do to get started is visit the website (**code.org**), which offers a range of high quality teaching and training materials for educators and students alike. An ideal starting place is the CS Fundamentals curriculum for elementary. It consists of four courses, each featuring 18–22 lessons that progress through stages of increasing difficulty. Concepts and skills are repeated throughout each course as students take a deeper dive each time they revisit a previously-taught skill. This chapter describes the four courses in the CS Fundamentals curriculum and offers advice on implementing specific lessons.

For young students who are pre-readers, start with Course 1. Course 2 builds from the concepts introduced in Course 1, but should be the starting point for second-graders or students who are reading. Course 3 is designed for students who have already taken Course 2, as this course digs deeper into the application of loops and conditionals and adds the concept of functions. Course 4 has been designed for use with students after they have completed both Course 2 and 3. Students will encounter increasing complexity and will have to combine their knowledge of multiple skills to complete the puzzles and tasks.

A blended learning environment exposes students to online activities, as well as "unplugged" leassons that can be done without a computer. These lessons take a kinesthetic approach to learning through the use of physical manipulatives to model computational concepts. The self-guided and self-paced tutorials make Code.org extremeley easy for first-time coding teachers to implement and flexible in application. For example, you might teach the course in consecutive days as a full unit, three times a week as a sub-unit, or even one day a week for 18 weeks.

Each course has links to lesson plans that are designed to take 25–50 minutes. Each lesson plan begins with an overview followed by a teaching summary that includes advice on getting started, the steps of the activity, a wrap-up activity, and an assessment portion. Each lesson also identifies new vocabulary and specific objectives presented in "Students will" statements that are easy to follow and assess. Teaching materials, resources, and prep lists (detailing what materials the students and teacher need for the lesson) are also included.

Since Code.org's lessons also integrate Common Core State Standards, teachers can easily align the lessons to what they are already teaching. The K–5 curriculum also aligns to CSTA and ISTE standards.

Course 1 Overview

The first course was developed for early readers and is recommended for ages four through six. Students will master use of a mouse or trackpad to input information into the computer. Exploring the sequencing of placing items in order, as well as identifying when things are not in order (debugging), is the main focus of this course. Tasks become increasingly complex as lessons move from completing simple puzzles to the sequential steps needed to complete a multi-step task. There are a total of 18 lessons. The following section will explore how teachers can implement a variety of these lessons into their curriculum.

Course 1 Exploration

Lessons 1 and 2 are "unplugged" lessons (lessons that do not require use of a computer) that have students determining which way the "Flurb" Code.org character will need to go by using directional arrows (Figure 9.1). These lessons build nicely upon the use of the Bee-Bots discussed in the previous section, as student understanding moves from the concrete buttons to the representational arrows. These two lessons focus on a variety of Common Core State Standards for speaking and listening. Throughout the lessons, students will be participating in collaborative

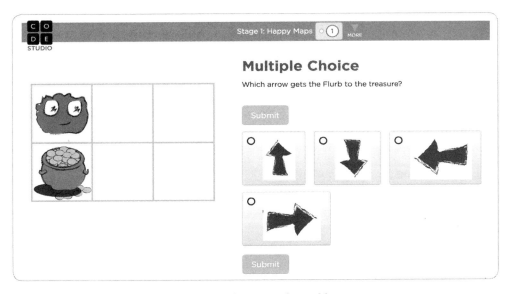

Figure 9.1. Code.org unplugged lesson.

conversations, confirming understanding (with details), and creating drawings that convey movement in symbolic instructions.

Along with literacy, the Common Core State Standards in Math focus on the kindergarten skills of geometry (**Math.Content.G.A.1**) and counting and cardinality (**Math. Content.K.CC.4**). Throughout the activities, students describe objects in their environment and their relative positions using terms such as "above," "below," "beside," "in front of," and "next to." They also apply their understanding of the relationship between numbers and quantities in a concrete modality.

Cardinal Directions

The video that introduces Lesson 4 does an excellent job of setting the stage for student success, with a kindergarten-age coder delivering the directions. This lesson introduces the cardinal directions of North, South, East, and West found in most state social studies standards. The lesson incorporates the characters from the popular game Angry Birds. Each maze provides students with the opportunity to program—by snapping coding blocks together—each move the Angry Bird makes.

Science Real Life Algorithms

Lesson 6 contains an unplugged lesson that helps students understand what an algorithm is through the act of planting a seed. This stage directly correlates to the following Next Generation Science Standard:

NGSS.K-LS1-1: Use observations to describe patterns of what plants and animals (including humans) need to survive.

In this lesson, students are reintroduced to the word "algorithm," defined as "a list of steps that you can follow to finish a task." To illustrate, students are asked to relate what they did to get ready for school that morning. The teacher facilitates the discussion by writing student responses on the board and helping the students put the steps in logical and sequential order. Next, students watch a video that demonstrates the "real life algorithm" of planting a seeed. The Code.org lesson provides a worksheet for a hands-on activity where students cut out squares of paper featuring the steps of planting a seed, then work to put them in order.

Teachers may be tempted to verify for students that their steps are in the correct order. Doing this causes students to miss out on critical learning. Letting students identify their mistakes and try again helps them develop perseverence and construct new learning pathways.

Science Sequences, Bees, and Honey

Lesson 7 uses sequencing as bees move to flowers, get nectar ,and then move to the honeycomb to make honey (Figure 9.2). There is a heavy cognitive lift that K–2 students are doing when completing these lessons, as they need to design a device (in this case, the coding blocks) to solve a problem. The specific Next Generation Science Standards teachers can incorporate into this coding lesson are:

NGSS.K-2-PS3-2: Use tools and materials provided to design and build a device that solves a specific problem or a solution to a specific problem.

NGSS.K-ESS3-1: Use a model to represent the relationship between the needs of different plants and animals (including humans) and the places they live.

These Code.org lessons are more meaningful when students bring their knowledge and understanding of bees into application, as they express the relationship between flowers and honey. Students will need to distinguish between flowers and honey as they create algorithms to successfully communicate the correct steps bees must take to get to a flower, gather the nectar, and place it in the honeycomb.

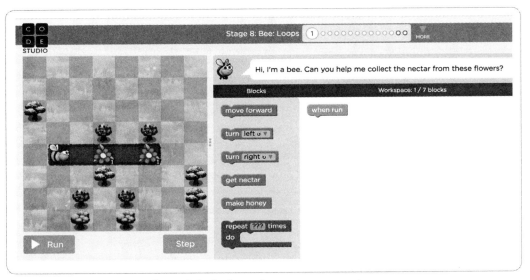

Figure 9.2. Code.org lesson on sequencing.

Error Analysis, Debugging, and Perseverence

Whether you are a using Bloom's taxonomy, Webb's DOK, or the Structure of the Observed Learning Outcome (SOLO) taxonomy, error analysis is an excellent opportunity for students to think at a higher level. Code.org does an excellent job of infusing intentional debugging exercises throughout their lessons. The skill of debugging helps students put into practice the Common Core State Standards Math Practice 3, which states "Construct viable arguments and critique the reasoning of others."

Lesson 5 uses the skills of debugging to help students critique the reasoning of others. The lesson begins with a video of a young gymnast, who explains the skill of debugging in other terms. She uses the example of correcting her hand placement on the balance beam to successfully complete a back handspring. In the lesson, once again using the familiar Angry Birds game characters, students are asked to analyze the code that is presented and change it to get the Angry Bird to the pig.

Lesson 9 is an unplugged lesson that focuses on the basis of Common Core State Standards Math Practice 1, which states, "Make sense of problems and persist in solving them." It's great for all K–5 classrooms as a stand-alone lesson on how to overcome frustration and persevere through a problem. This lesson can be done with gumdrops and toothpicks, marshmallows and popsicle sticks (or spaghetti), or even simple paper and tape.

With the use of technology, another variation of this project is to repeat the process each year, from kindergarten through fifth grade. Since the focus of building a strong foundation is part of the Next Generation Science Standards for Engineering Practice, watch as students demonstrate their perseverence in improving their designs year after year. As they engage with this performance task, discuss how their thinking changes as they acquire more knowledge and skills.

Literacy *Building Stories with Coding Blocks*

Lesson 16 will allow students to put the pieces together and begin building their own simple stories. The ability to select a character and the introduction of the "say" block allows for students to create an interactive story. During the lesson, the following blocks are introduced:

- **"set mood"** allows the character to be happy, neutral, angry, or sad

- **"when characters move next to each other"** allows actions to happen when the characters are next to each other

- **"show"** makes characters appear on the screen

- **"set background"** allows user to select a different background scene

- **"set speed"** determines how fast a character moves

- **"play sound"** allows students to play preselected sounds

- **"vanish"** makes a character disappear from the screen

In order to complete these stages, students read simple directions— for example, "Make the dog move to the cat and say 'hello' when he gets there." For non-readers, there is an icon for them to select which will read the directions to them. Since the focus of this lesson is on creating a story, many of the Common Core State Standards in Literacy can be used for evaluation.

Digital Citizenship and Safety

Lesson 17 is an unplugged lesson that has a great video explaining internet safety for students. The video outlines three main rules:

- Ask your parents first.

- Only talk to people you know.

- Stick to places just right for you.

The lesson with this stage reviews the process of how to create a username that is safe. This lesson aligns directly to the ISTE Standards for Students Standard 2, Digital Citizen, which states, "Students recognize the rights, responsibilities and opportunities of living, learning and working in an interconnected digital world, and they act and model in ways that are safe, legal and ethical" (ISTE, 2016).

Course 2 Overview

Code.org Course 2 should be the starting point for students who can read but have no prior coding experience. Students will begin with a more advanced introduction to the cardinal directions and moving with arrows. The recommneded grade range for this course is grades 2 through 5. There are a total of 19 lessons in this course that can be incorporated into the curriculum in a variety of ways, as the following sections will show.

Course 2 Exploration

The focus of Lesson 1 is on the Engineering Design standards of the Next Generation Science Standards. In this unplugged lesson, students pretend they are an Automatic Realization Machine (ARM) and using graph paper they recreate a drawing their classmates have in front of them by following commands.

  ### *Loops*

Lessons 5 through 8 introduce the programming concept of loops through a dance activity. This is the perfect lesson for focusing on Common Core State Standard Mathematical Practice 8, which states, "Look for and express regularity in repeated reasoning. In this standard, mathematically proficient students notice if calculations are repeated and they look for shortcuts."

In computer programming, the word "loop" means the action of doing something over and over again. Lesson 5 begins with an unplugged activity that will get students up and dancing. The students are provided with a worksheet that shows the steps of "The Iteration," a series of dance moves that are repeated three times (Figure 9.3). Teachers have the students run through the dance slowly, one instruction at a time in order to identify the loop.

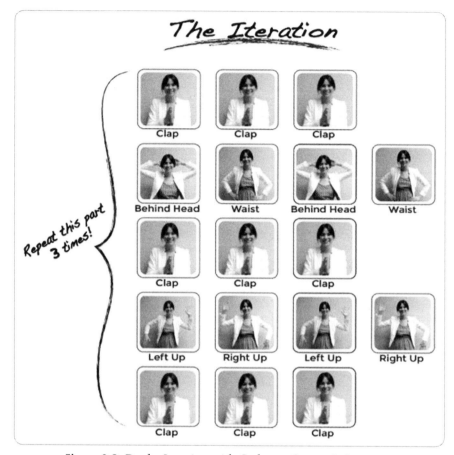

Figure 9.3. Do the Iteration with Code.org Course 2: Lesson 5

 ### *Conditionals*

Lesson 12 is where students will explore conditionals. Conditional statements are covered in both literacy and math standards and the understanding of conditionals is important, especially in the area of geometry.

CCSS.Math.Content.3.G.A.1: Understand that shapes in different categories (e.g., rhombuses, rectangles, and others) may share attributes (e.g., having four sides), and that the shared attributes can define a larger category (e.g., quadrilaterals). Recognize rhombuses, rectangles, and squares as examples of quadrilaterals, and draw examples of quadrilaterals that do not belong to any of these subcategories.

Conditionals can be used to identify quadrilaterals using "if..., then..." statements like the following.

If the shape has four sides, **then** it is a parallelogram. (FALSE)

If the shape has two pairs of parallel lines, **then** it is a parallelogram. (TRUE)

There is a wonderful resource at CK-12.org for "if.., then..." statements that teachers can use to help students revisit this concept (**www.ck12.org/geometry/ If-Then-Statements**). I say revisit because as infants and toddlers, children rely on "if..., then..." reasoning to learn how to walk, talk, and run. Children quickly learn that if they say the word "up," then the adult will follow suit and pick them up.

Lesson 13 will challenge students as it allows them to participate in lessons with the bees that practice using loops of "repeat ...times" and conditionals where the students will need let the bee move to the flower and then decide "if nectar = 1" then the bee will "get nectar." Encourage students to persevere through their frustration, as the coding during this lesson can be quite complex for second- through fourth-graders. Allow your talented coders and higher level math thinkers to help support other students, and even the teacher, during this lesson.

(Literacy) ## *Interactive Games and Digital Storytelling*

If you would like to have students use Code.org to build their own interactive game, then Lesson 17 could be used a stand-alone lesson for students in grades 2 through 5. In exercises 1 through 10, students are shown how to use a variety of coding blocks that will help them understand how to make actors speak, move, say things when the approach eachother, and play sounds.

After reviewing all of these skills, the students create their own story. This Code. org lesson is a fun and interactive way to teach the following narrative writing standards:

ELA-Literacy.W.2.3: Write narratives in which they recount a well-elaborated event or short sequence of events, include details to describe actions, thoughts, and feelings, use temporal words to signal event order, and provide a sense of closure.

ELA-Literacy.W.3.3 ,W.4.3, and W.5.3: Write narratives to develop real or imagined experiences or events using effective technique, descriptive details, and clear event sequences.

The best part of the lesson is that it offers a quick and easy way for students to share their stories with parents and other. Once completed and saved, the student simply enters the U.S. phone number for the person they would like to send their story to. A text message is sent via Twilio and the recipient simply clicks on the link to see the story. The following link features a short sample story that was created for this book: **studio.code.org/c/387769868**.

Course 3 Overview

Course 3 is designed for students who have successfully completed Course 2. Students in this course will further explore programming topics that have already been introduced in order to create flexible solutions to more complex problems. This course is recommended for grades 4 and 5 and engages student creativity, as students create interactive games and stories they can share with others. There are a total of 22 lessons in this course. The following sections will explore how teachers can implement a variety of these lessons into their curriculum.

Course 3 Exploration

This course begins with an unplugged lesson that introduces students to computational thinking. There is a heavy emphasis on the **Common Core Mathematical Practice 7**, "Look for and make use of structure." Within this lesson, Code.org focuses on four components of computational thinking: decomposition, patterns, abstraction, and algorithms. The lesson simplifies the process of solving complex problems by first breaking the problem into smaller pieces (decomposition). Students then look for similarities, followed by finding differences (patterns). Once these deifferences are identified and removed (abstraction), students can finally put the steps in order (algorithms) and begin to create new problems that follow the same pattern.

NOTE: Lesson 2 has zombies and may be a bit scary for some younger children.

 Math

Shapes and Perimeter

For those of us who remember the days of the Logo turtle, Lesson 3 focuses on drawing a variety of shapes. This is a great lesson to use for the fourth grade Common Core State Standard **4.MD.A.3**, which states, "Apply the area and perimeter formulas for rectangles in real world and mathematical problems." While the main focus is on perimeter, the following standards can be seen in application as students complete the various drawings using code.

Math.Content.4.MD.C.5: Recognize angles as geometric shapes that are formed wherever two rays share a common endpoint, and understand concepts of angle measurement.

Math.Content. 4.MD.C.7: Recognize angle measure as additive.

Math.Content.4.G.A.1: Draw points, lines, line segments, rays, angles (right, acute, obtuse), and perpendicular and parallel lines.

Math.Content.4.G.A.3: Recognize a line of symmetry for a two-dimensional figure as a line across the figure such that the figure can be folded along the line into matching part.

The artist in Lesson 3 draws some complex pictures based on advanced mathematical concepts. This can be a great lesson for more advanced math students..

Lessons 5 and 6 allow students to practice these skills by drawing a variety of computer generated shapes. (*Note:* Lesson 4 in the Art and Science section uses an unplugged activity to help students develop a concrete understanding of a function.)

These lessons help students to understand the following mathematics standard.

Math.Content.4.MD.C.5.A: An angle is measured with reference to a circle with its center at the common endpoint of the rays, by considering the fraction of the circular arc between the points where the two rays intersect the circle. An angle that turns through 1/360 of a circle is called a "one- degree angle," and can be used to measure angles.

While second- and third-graders will understand the purpose of a function during these lessons, it is important that teachers intentionally help fourth grade students make the connection between the degrees turned in each angle and the angle measures equally 360 degrees for each shape.

Variables and Functions

In Lesson 4, variables and functions are made concrete through the use of an unplugged activity on creating functional suncatchers. Within the Code.org lesson plan is a video that explains the lesson in detail. This aides in understanding, especially for K–5 teachers who may not be familiar with these terms.

This unplugged activity can meet the Next Generation Science and Engineering Practices in grades 3-5:

Engineering.Design.3-5-ETS1-2: Generate and compare multiple possible solutions to a problem based on how well each is likely to meet the criteria and constraints of the problem.

If all students are provided with the same supplies (criteria or variables) and the constraints (use of variables to create skill sets) remain consistent and expected, the final products (suncatchers) generated can be compared for multiple possible solutions. This lesson also covers art integration, as students are creating an artistic representation of their computer program.

(Literacy) *Algorithms and Expository Writing*

Lesson 10 has students playing with dice in an unplugged lesson to build the concrete understanding of algorithms. They discover algorithms are behind almost everything we do, from getting up in the morning and getting ready for school, to the after-school activities the student participates in. This is a great place to tie in expository writing and having students write out the steps needed to make a peanut butter and jelly sandwich.

This activity is often one that teachers will use in teaching Common Core State Standards in Writing for grades 3-5, such as **ELA-Literacy.W.3**, "Write informative/explanatory texts to examine a topic and convey ideas and information clearly."

The one addition that needs to be added to these expository writing pieces is identifying which steps are repeated and then looking through the lens of computer science and how a computer would efficiently run the functions of the program. A full lesson with alignment to computational thinking can be found at **Nofearcoding.org**.

Digital Citizenship

Code.org expands upon the 2016 ISTE Standards for Students Standard 2 with more information on the internet, crowdsourcing, and digital citizenship. Through unplugged activities, students will act out how the internet works by demonstrating how messages are received across the internet. Comparisons of traditional "snail mail" to the current use of email helps student understanding. Crowdsourcing is demonstrated with a deck of cards, explaining how completing a task with a group of friends can be easier than going it alone. Finally, digital citizenship is explored with the use of superheroes instilling the importance of being safe, responsible, and respectful.

Course 4 Overview

Highlights of Course 4 include unplugged activities on tangrams, Mad Glibs (similar to Madlibs), dice games, meteorology, songwriting, and binary images. This course is designed for students who have successfully completed both Courses 2 and 3. Students will learn how to tackle puzzles with increased complexity as they learn how to combine several of the skills they have learned in the previous two courses. Mathematics contained within this course are most appropriate for grades 4 and 5, with some lessons that will challenge even the most advanced math students. There are a total of 22 lessons contained in this course. The following sections will explore how teachers can implement a variety of these lessons into their curriculum.

Course 4 Exploration

Literacy *Create Abstract Art with Shapes*

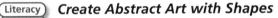

Lesson 1 is an unplugged lesson that provides students with concrete manipulatives (tangrams) that are used to recreate a specific algorithm card that one player tries to describe to the other players. Some shapes are simple, while others are more complex.

The following Common Core Language Arts Standards can be assessed during this lesson.

> **ELA-Literacy.L.3.6:** Acquire and use accurately grade-appropriate conversational, general academic, and domain-specific words and phrases, including those that signal spatial and temporal relationships.

> **ELA-Literacy.L.5.6:** Acquire and use accurately grade-appropriate general academic and domain- specific words and phrases, including those that signal contrast, addition, and other logical relationships.

ART APPLICATION

Art teachers can easily incorporate this lesson by using a coloring by number for younger students and having older students create abstract art with tangram shapes. Art teachers can use this lesson multiple years, as their skills of orally describing and explaining continue to grow! For more advanced students, art teachers can show the following video: What Tangrams Can Teach You About Design Fundamentals (**youtu.be/c-9O3tNokic**).

Nested Loops

Nested loops (a loop inside of another repeated loop) are reviewed in Lesson 3. Students can make connections with attributes of shapes, as well as angle measures (30-60-90 degree triangles), and calculate the number of degrees needed to create a variety of shapes. Puzzle 12 is extremely challenging and will take trial and error as well as perseverance to find the solution.

Puzzle 12 focuses on the following Common Core Math Standards and Practice:

> **Math.Content.4.MD.C.5:** Recognize angles as geometric shapes that are formed whenever two rays share a common endpoint, and understand the concepts of angle measurement.

> **Mathematical Practice 6:** Attend to precision
> (For a deeper look at the Standards for Mathematical Practice and how they relate to computational thinking, refer to Appendix B of this book.)

When using trial and error methods, students are working on attending to precision. In the exploration of the solution, student must be exact in their measurements of pixels and degrees.

Variables and Patterns

Lesson 6 introduces variables, a key concept in Common Core Math Standards for operations and algebraic thinking, particularly standard **Math.Content.OA.C5**, which states, "Generate a number or shape pattern that follows a given rule. Identify apparent features of the pattern that were not explicit in the rule itself."

In this lesson, the shape pattern created by the rule is a triangle. An apparent feature of the pattern that is not explicit of the rule itself is represented by the last block of the program.

Loops and Weather Forecasting

Lesson 8 explains the importance of using for loops in the scientific field of meteorology. A "for loop" is a loop that has a pre-specified beginning, end, and increment (step interval). Computerized weather forecasting models are used to predict patterns that are essential, in the running of wind farms, for energy. Thus, the focus of this lesson could also be a stand-alone lesson for those students who demonstrate advanced understanding of mathematics and/or logic thinking. This lesson also incorporates the following Next Generation Science Standard.

NGSS.ETS2.B: Influence of engineering, technology, and science on society and the natural world.

How do science, engineering, and the technologies that result from them affect the ways in which people live? How do they affect the natural world? Over time, people's needs and wants change, as do their demands for new and improved technologies. Engineers improve existing technologies or develop new ones to increase their benefits (e.g., better artificial limbs), to decrease known risks (e.g., seatbelts in cars), and to meet societal demands (e.g., cell phones). When new technologies become available, they can bring about changes in the way people live and interact with one another.

This lesson focuses on the fact that we need computers to repeat things a certain number of times, but we also want to keep track of the values as we do.

The mathematics involved in this lesson still use basic line measures and the knowledge of angles and degrees of turns; however, the logic thinking needed for understanding for loops can be quite complex. Exposure to these concepts will help students begin their understanding of limits that are used in high school mathematics.

Encouraging risk-taking and exploring this concept with students can be an empowering experience. No fear coding means branching out and allowing students to explore concepts that they might understand, even though teachers do not. Allow the students to help you in finding the understanding and application of concepts in these lessons!

Teaching Parameters with Music

Lesson 13 uses the example of ice cream to teach about parameters. If each ice cream cone has a topping, the topping is the function. Each different kind of topping that can go on top of the ice cream would be the parameters; thus creating a variety of parameters that are possible. Functions and parameters work together to create great computer programs... and sundaes too!

Music teachers can easily incorporate this lesson by introducing the concepts with a familiar song that almost all children know, *Old McDonald Had a Farm*.

The chorus of the song identifies the parameters. In this case, the parameters are the 'Animal Name' and the 'Sound' the animal makes. By substituting in 'cow' for 'animal name' and 'moo' for 'sound,' you have the full chorus of the song that students can sing. This unplugged lesson then asks students to create their own chorus and identify the parameters.

Music teachers could have a lot of fun with this activity by allowing for the creativity of original student compositions.

Back in the classroom, after the music teacher covers the meaning of parameters, students can then apply these skills to various coding puzzles in lessons 14 through 16.

CHAPTER 10

Code.org in the Classroom— Case Studies

Code.org offers lessons that can be easily mapped to content or standards along with a lesson plans and assessment and extension resources. The following case studies are just a few examples of how teachers have implemented Code.org course lessons and the Hour of Code activities within their classrooms. From unplugged lessons to highly engaging Disney and Minecraft-themed activities, there is something for everyone. Start by trying out one of the following lessons or check out **Nofearcoding.org** to connect with others who are implementing Code.org in their classrooms.

Code with Anna and Elsa

The Code.org lesson Code with Anna and Elsa can be tied directly to fourth grade Common Core State Standards in Mathematics. Throughout this coding exploration, students make observations and measure the distances and angles that construct the various fractals.

(Math)

Code with Anna and Elsa
Website: hourofcode.com/frzn
Grades: 2 and up
Description: Let's use code to join Anna and Elsa as they explore the magic and beauty of ice. You will create snowflakes and patterns as you ice-skate and make a winter wonderland that you can then share with your friends!

Math.Content.4.MD.C.6: Measure angles in whole-number degrees using a protractor. Sketch angles of specified measure.

In order to help students make connections to the degrees in each of the angles that are needed to construct the shapes, the author created a prompting guide of questions to ask students as they work through each of the puzzles in the lesson.

PUZZLE	MATHEMATICAL QUESTIONS TO ASK:
1	What did you notice when you pushed the Run button?
2	How many degrees did you need to turn?
3	How many 90-degree turns did you need to make to complete the square?
4	How many times did you need to repeat the pattern?
5	How many times did you repeat the pattern? Why did you need to repeat the pattern that many times? How many degrees did you need to turn? Does it matter if you turn right or left?
6	How many "repeat" commands did you need to use? What did the blocks do that repeated 4 times? What did the blocks do that repeated 10 times?
7	Why is it important that Elsa is able to move forward and backward to create this shape?
8 & 9	Why is each turn in this fractal 36 degrees? Four degrees?
10	What is the difference between a rectangle or square and this parallelogram?

A full student worksheet for this lesson can be found at **Nofearcoding.org.**

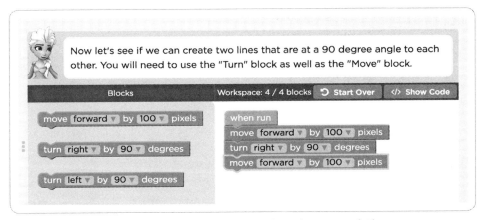

Figure 10.1. Code.org lesson Code with Anna and Elsa.

Throughout the 20 puzzles in this coding activity, students progressively encounter fractals that are more difficult to instruct. Most students can successfully complete Puzzle 11, with some students persevering through Puzzle 12. When students discovered that they could send their drawings to their parents' phone once completed, motivation increased.

Beading Variables and Functions

Functional Suncatchers
Website: studio.code.org/s/course3/stage/4/puzzle/1

Teacher Vivian Chow has used this Code.org lesson to physically explore fuctions and variables while having her students make suncatchers, or as they call them, "backpack charms" using ribbons, beads, and spacers. The unplugged activity requires students to string together a pattern of objects then make programming instructions for the pattern. Along the way, they are able to talk about the term "ambiguous" (being unclear). In Figure 10.2, you can see a finished charm with the objects (variables) labeled

For this activity, the string of items is the "program." The different items (beads, spacers, knots, etc.) are the "variables." According to the definition, a variable is a placeholder for a piece of information that can change.

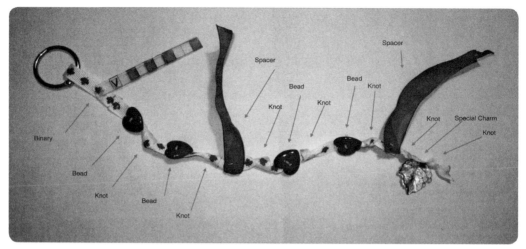

Figure 10.2. Backpack charm with different "variables" labeled.

Ms. Chow challenged her students to figure out a way of grouping together parts of the sequence and renaming it so they wouldn't need to write down so many variables. This grouping together of instructions is what is called a "function." As an example, we could group numbers 2, 3, and 4, and rename this a function called "Skills-1." Instead of writing "bead, knot, bead," we can create a function for this grouping, which is the exact same thing but in "short-hand" form.

Ms. Chow thought this step would be quite straightforward—her students range from ages 9 to 17—but in fact, it took quite a lot of arguing and many tries before they could make the program contain the fewest lines. They talked about efficiency along the way, which would be the most stream-lined piece of coding, or the program that needs the fewest lines.

Ms. Chow taught the lesson and students wrote out the program on one day, then did the beading on the following day.

Younger students could do this with pipe-cleaners. If you don't want to involve sewing, you could use charms that have larger holes to string them through. However, Ms. Chow does point out that there was a bonus in that her boys learned how to sew a button down! It was a fun activity and you can see students walking around the school with their creations hanging from their backpacks.

Make Music with Scratch

More than just playing sounds, Scratch can play the individual notes and chords of instruments. Musically-inclined students love to compose their own music using this open-source program. To get started, you can go to the Hour of Code and select this Hour of Code activity. A video accompanying the activity will walk you through your first musical experience.

Make Music with Scratch
Grades: 2–8
Website: hourofcode.com/scratchmus
Description: With Scratch, you can create your own interactive games, stories, and animations, and share them with your friends. To get started, make an interactive music project. Activity cards and a workshop guide are also available for free on scratch.mit.edu.

After exploring the Hour of Code activity above, I overheard my class discussing reading projects they were working on. In working with my team's reading teachers, I discovered they were working on characters and setting. We began using Google's Computer Science Activity 7 to explore how music can change the feelings of character and the setting.

ELA-Literacy.RL.3.3: Describe characters in a story (e.g., their traits, motivations, or feelings) and explain how their actions contribute to the sequence of events.

ELA-Literacy.RL.4.3: Describe in depth a character, setting, or event in a story or drama, drawing on specific details in the text (e.g., a character's thoughts, words, or actions).

ITCH Bouncing Ball

ITCH Bouncing Ball
Website: hourofcode.com/itchbounceball

In looking through the Hour of Code resources, I found "The Bouncing Ball" by ITCH. After watching the short videos that go with this project, students in my enrichment class found that by adding a few simple items, they could create a game that would help them predict future motion.

NGSS.3-PS2-2: Make observations and/or measurements of an object's motion to provide evidence that a pattern can be used to predict future motion.

The tutorial had students using a "sprite" that was a ball, but students also had to add a paddle by drawing a think line. Students then placed the paddle in the center of the screen and added a few scripts to the original program. We added that if the ball was touching the color of the paddle, it would point in a specific direction. Students then made observations of what occurred when different directions were set.

Students recorded their observations on a chart. For students who caught on to the patterns early, we allowed for open exploration. Students explored by changing the number of steps, changing the number of degrees, and starting the ball from a specific location. It was amazing to watch the things that students tried, and they were interested in what their classmates were trying. Inspired by their explorations, we decided to make a classroom chart that had two columns: What I Tried, and What Happened, after which we discussed cause and effect.

Incorporate Scratch Across the Curriculum

Scratch is a free visual programming language developed by the MIT (Massachusetts Institute of Technology) Media Lab. This drag-and-drop environment of visual lego- looking blocks is used by students, scholars, teachers and parents to easily create animations, games, and stories. It provides a stepping stone to the more advanced world of computer programming. This section explores some of the available resources Scratch offers for K–5 educators. You will learn

- Why teachers should use a visual programming language
- How to get started wtih Scratch
- What teaching with Scratch looks like

CHAPTER

11

Why Teach Coding and Computational Thinking with Scratch

The visual block programming language Scratch is ideal for introducing K–5 students to coding. Scratch (scratch.mit.edu) was developed by Mitchel Resnick and others at the in the Lifelong Kindergarten research group at the Massachusetts Institute of Technology (MIT) Media Lab. The language was named "Scratch" after "scratching," the technique used by DJs to produce distinctive sounds by moving a vinyl record back and forth on a turntable. With Scratch, the user takes different bits of code contained within colored blocks and snaps them together to create something new. The action is not unlike snapping together LEGO blocks, making it an extremely easy user interface and one that appeals to young students.

There are a lot of visual programming languages out there (Table 11.1), so why use Scratch? Coding is all about trial and error so trying other programming languages is encouraged. Following are some reasons why Scratch makes a great entry point for teaching with coding.

Easy to Use and Free

Scratch, unlike other programming languages, is designed first and foremost for kids, making it very easy to learn and use. Users can see instant results without needing to be versed in the language of code. As they grow more familiar, they can "read" the code within the blocks.

Best of all, Scratch is free! You don't need a license to use Scratch in your school, at home, or anywhere else. The development and maintenance of Scratch is paid for by grants and donations from the National Science Foundation, Google, the LEGO Foundation, Intel, and others.

TABLE 11.1. Guide to Visual Programming Languages

LANGUAGE	WEBSITE	COMMENTS
Snap!	snap.berkeley.edu	Limited "sprites" to choose from More advanced programming blocks Build Your Own Blocks advanced programming
Tynker	www.tynker.com	Lots of fun and creative sprites Lessons already created Fee based
Blockly	developers.google.com/blockly	JavaScript appears side-by-side with blocks No characters or sounds
stencyl	www.stencyl.com	Download software on computer Only basic package is free Advanced programming options
Hopscotch	www.gethopscotch.com	Only for iPad or iPhone Fee based program Fewer features than Scratch

Table continues on following page.

LANGUAGE	WEBSITE	COMMENTS
ScratchJr	www.scratchjr.org	iPads and Android tablets Free Designed for ages 5–7 and non-readers
Kodable	www.kodable.com	Standards aligned Some lessons free, some fee based Designed for K–5 schools
Kudo	www.kodugamelab.com	Must be downloaded Games can be played on a PC and Xbox Free

Access a Worldwide Educational Community

Scratch is not just for kids or teens; teachers and adults can use Scratch to create effective educational tools such as math quizzes, physics simulations, and educational videos. The website Scratch ED (scratched.gse.harvard.edu), supported by Harvard University, has resources for teachers including a variety of educational levels, content types, curricular areas, and languages. Content types include: activities, assessments, curriculum, handouts, lesson plans, presentations, reference guides, research, sample projects, textbooks, tools, tutorials, and websites.

The Scratch community has more than 16 million registered users and over 20 million projects shared by users. It is a global community of learners, with over 7 million users in the United States. Statistics are collected with real-time data at scratch.mit.edu/statistics. You can view monthly activity trends, traffic, active users, project shares, scratch block usage, and even the age distribution of new "Scratchers."

Computational Thinking Made Visible

Programming requires students to use cognitive and metacognitive strategies linked to computational thinking. Among the strategies used are thinking sequentially, exploring cause and effect, persevering through problem solving, and understanding design thinking in application. Scratch is hands-on and highly engaging, as students manipulate "sprites" (characters) and code blocks to create original content. The process is open-ended—as there are myriad ways to make characters move, speak, and interact—and allows students to learn about math and language in a meaningful and motivating context.

In an article published in the journal *Communications of the ACM* (Association for Computing Machinery) titled "Scratch: Programming for All," the researchers recognize that it has become commonplace to refer to young people as "digital natives" due to their use of and fluency with technology. It recognizes that many young people are comfortable sending and receiving text messages, playing online games and browsing the web; but the researchers question if this really makes them fluent, as few are able to create their own games, simulations or animations. They create an analogy of students being able to "read" but not "write." (Resnick, Silverman, Kafai, et. al., 2009)

If digital fluency means being able to design, create and invent with new media, Scratch is an excellent tool in making this kind of thinking visible. More importantly, programming supports computational thinking. Using Scratch helps students to learn important problem-solving and design strategies that carry over to non-programming domains. It provides opportunities for students to reflect on their own thinking, and even to think about thinking itself, as students work to find errors within their thinking and then correct those errors to make their games work.

In the process of making student thinking visible, Scratch has also created a personalized project based platform that allows students to import pictures and music clips, as well as record voices and create graphics. This highly personalized, visible thinking can capture the growth of computational thinking skills over time.

Metacognition

Flavell (1979) described metacognition as the interplay between goals (what the learner is trying to achieve), strategies (how the learner tries to achieve it), metacognitive knowledge (what the learner knows about learning), and metacognitive experiences (how the learner thinks about that knowledge in action). The significance of metacognition in a variety of learning and cognitive processes has long been recognized.

Metacognition plays an important role in oral communication of information, oral persuasion, oral comprehension, reading comprehension, writing, language acquisition, attention, memory, problem solving, social cognition, and, various types of self-control and self-instruction. (Flavell, 1979) The ideas of self-control and self-instruction described by Flavell—varyingly referred to as self-control, self-instruction, self-regulation, self-efficacy, and self-directedness—speak directly to the idea of learner agency. Bandura highlighted the significance of these capacities, for supporting learning as both a life-long and life-wide activity. Development of capabilities for self-directedness enables individuals not only to continue their intellectual growth beyond their formal education but to advance the nature and quality of their life pursuits. Changing realities are placing a premium on the capability for self-directed learning throughout the life span. The rapid pace of technological change and the accelerated growth of knowledge require continual upgrading of competencies if people are to survive and prosper under increasingly competitive conditions. (Bandura, 1997)

Metacognition has been shown to increase student ability in the area of problem solving, which is useful when programming in Scratch. Teachers can help to facilitate this thinking by engaging students in metacognition, or thinking about their thinking, by

asking students a variety of questions such as:

- What was your biggest challenge throughout this project? Can you remember what you were thinking when you faced this challenge?

- Are there different ways to make a character move? How did you identify the different ways?

- What would you do differently if you had more time?

- How do you think your thinking would have changed if you had to work with a partner?

How to Teach Using Scratch

It's time to move beyond the early adopters and participate as computational creators! Scratch was designed so users can explore and "tinker" with programming concepts without fear of missing a key punctuation mark, rendering their creation useless. The first step should be to visit the Scratch website (**scratch.mit.edu**), create an account, and being playing with the concepts in this section.

Setting up a Scratch Teacher Account

Anyone can create a Scratch account by entering their email and choosing a username and password. You can also request a teacher account, which makes it easier to create accounts for groups of students. Additional features within teacher accounts allow you to manage student participation, organize student projects, and monitor comments.

To request a teacher account, go to the Scratch for Educators page at **scratch. mit.edu/educators** and click the button "Request Teacher Account." The website includes a teacher account FAQ and a video. Once your request has been submitted, the approval process can take up to a day. Then you will be up and running and ready to begin using Scratch with your students.

> Scratch has a help page (**scratch.mit.edu/help/**) that includes a step-by-step "Getting Started Guide," Scratch activity cards, and a variety of video tutorials.

Getting Oriented

The Scratch interface is designed to be user friendly. Here is a brief "tour" for new users. The screen (or project editor, shown in Figure 12.1) is divided into sections:

The Stage Area is where you see the actions resulting from the code. Consider Scratch to be like a school play. The stage is where you will see the programming running, as the actors on the stage perform. You will see the characters (in this example, the Scratch cat) moving, talking, and interacting here.

The Code Area is where you will drag and drop the programming blocks. Consider the code area to be like a piece of paper. This is where you are writing your code.

The Sprites Area is where you can import, draw or select your characters.

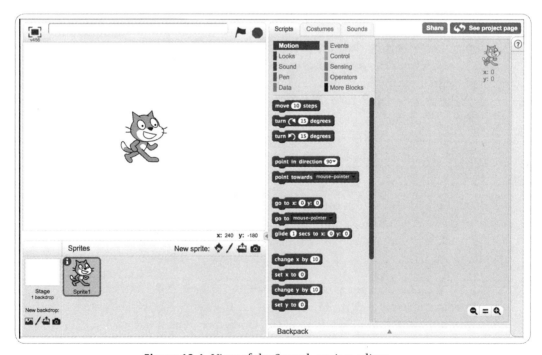

Figure 12.1. View of the Scratch project editor.

Consider the Sprites characters of your story. Each Sprite will have its own code to perform on the stage. You can select from a variety of pre-loaded Sprites, import an image from your computer, or create your own Sprites within Scratch.

Scratch Studio

A Scratch studio is a place where multiple users can store projects for group access. The studios are one way to collect and organize Scratch projects online. With a teacher account, you can create a class studio where students can share their projects.

Try it! Introduce yourself to the No Fear Coding Studio by creating a "remix" of one of the projects in the studio.

1. Sign in to your Scratch account.
2. Go to the No Fear Coding Studio using this link: **scratch.mit.edu/studios/3801060/**
3. Open one of the projects in the studio.
4. Click on the "See Inside" button.
5. Click on the "Remix" button.
6. Customize your project to introduce yourself.

Click on the "Add projects" button and your shared projects will show up at the bottom of the page under the "Add Projects" bar. Use the arrows to find your project and then click "Add +" to add your project to the No Fear Coding–STRETCh Instructor Introductions Studio.

Computational Thinking: Scratch in Application

Let's take a closer look at how Scratch integrates with computational thinking skills. Table 12.1 is the same chart that appeared in Chapter 2 with one added one component, how computational thinking applies directly to the application of Scratch when used for student projects.

TABLE 12.1. Computational Thinking Concepts Applied to Scratch

ISTE / CSTA COMPUTATIONAL THINKING CONCEPTS	DEFINITION	SCRATCH IN APPLICATION
Simulation	Representation or model of a process. Simulation also involves running experiments using models.	Your Scratch project
Problem Decomposition	Breaking down tasks into smaller, manageable parts	Planning out your Scratch game. Gathering images, sounds, characters
Abstraction	Reducing complexity to define main idea	Making sure all the tasks meet the purpose of the project
Algorithms & Procedures	Series of ordered steps taken to solve a problem or achieve some end	Determining the types and order of Scratch blocks needed
Data Collection	The process of gathering appropriate information	Putting the Scratch blocks together
Automation	Having computers or machines do repetitive or tedious tasks	Looking for efficiency within the use of blocks (loops)
Data Analysis	Making sense of data, finding patterns, and drawing conclusions	Running the program. Finding errors

| Data Representation | Depicting and organizing data in appropriate graphs, charts, words or images | Fixing errors to make sure program runs correctly |
| Parallelization | Organizing resources to simultaneously carry out tasks reach a common goal | Making sure that items correctly run at the same time when needed |

Now that you understand the "big picture" of how Scratch fits into computational thinking, let's look a bit closer at the algorithm and procedures used within Scratch. Table 12.2 presents a set of computational concepts that are common in many programming languages. These seven concepts (which fall under the computational thinking category of Algorithms and Procedures) are used in many Scratch projects and can be transferred to other programming and non-programming applications.

Table 12.2 explains how each of the algorithms and procedures can be used within Scratch and identifies the Scratch blocks one might use to demonstrate the concept.

TABLE 12.2. Algorithms and Procedures Used within Scratch

ALGORITHMS & PROCEDURES	HOW ARE THE CONCEPTS USED?	EXAMPLE SCRATCH BLOCKS
Sequence	When we give students multi-step directions to follow, we are asking them to follow a sequence of steps.	move 10 steps wait 1 secs move 10 steps wait 1 secs

Loops	When a set of directions need to be followed over and over again, we can use programming blocks to repeat the process.	repeat 10
		  move 10 steps
		  wait 1 secs
		  move 10 steps
		  wait 1 secs

Table continues on following page.

ALGORITHMS & PROCEDURES	HOW ARE THE CONCEPTS USED?	EXAMPLE SCRATCH BLOCKS
Events	When one thing causes another to happen. In Scratch, the most commonly used block is the "green flag." When the student clicks on the green flag, the scripts (or programming blocks) will begin to play in order (from top to bottom).	
Parallelism	This is when sequences of instructions are happening at the same time. For example, if you want to have a sprite talk while moving or move to music, you would need to have two separate events going on simultaneously.	
Conditionals	This is when blocks are used to make decisions based on certain conditions. For example, if the cat is touching the fish, he will say "Meow."	
Operators	These are used to support mathematical, logical, and string expressions. For the purposes of K–5 teachers, we will focus on only mathematical and logical thinking.	

Data	Data involves storing, retrieving, and updating values. Scratch currently uses variables and lists. For the purposes of K–5 teachers, we will focus on the variable "score," as keeping score is a frequent motivator for young game designers.	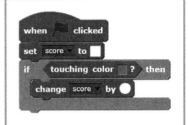

Coding with Scratch: Practices & Perspectives

Harvard Graduate School of Education students Brennan, Balch & Chung (2015) created a creative computing curriculum guide for teachers. They are members of the ScratchEd research team and revised the Creative Computing Guide released in 2011, as well as incorporated feedback from the 2013 Creative Computing Online Workshop. This guide can be accessed on the **Nofearcoding.org** website or by going to **goo.gl/VnPDLi**.

Within this guide, the authors state that creative computing is not only about coding, but also about creativity and empowerment. This is an important part of the "how" in using Scratch. Allowing students to be creative and draw upon their imagination and interests when creating projects is an essential part of the 21st century skills needed for future employment. It also emphasizes the knowledge, practices, and fundamental literacies needed to create they types of interactive media that engage students.

As you begin exploring Scratch and implementing it into your curriculum content, consider the observations of research into this topic. Brennan & Resnick (2012) used artifact-based interviews to study the development of computational thinking in interactive media design. Although the young people they interviewed had utilized a variety of strategies, four main sets of practices became apparent. These practices focus on the process of thinking and learning, moving beyond the "what" you are learning to "how" you are learning.

> **Experimenting and iterating:** Developing a little bit, trying it out, then developing a bit more
>
> **Testing and debugging:** Making sure things work and finding and solving problems when they arise
>
> **Reusing and remixing:** Making something by building on existing projects or ideas

Abstracting and modularizing: Exploring connections between the whole and the parts

In their interviews and conversations with Scratchers, Brennan & Resnick (2012) heard young designers describe evolving understandings of themselves, their relationships to others, and the navigation of the technological world around them. Thus, the dimension of perspective was added to their computational thinking framework. The three elements that are listed represent the shifts in perspective that were observed in young coders.

Expressing: Realizing that computation is a medium of creation. "I can create."

Connecting: Recognizing the power of creating with and for others. "I can do different things when I have access to others."

Questioning: Feeling empowered to ask questions about the world. "I can (use computation to) ask questions to make sense of (computational things in) the world."

This content has been put together to intentionally scaffold the learning of computational thinking at the most basic level. Once students understand the language, they will be able to apply their knowledge to a variety of projects and content knowledge. Instead of having students create a presentation on Google Slides or PowerPoint, let them code their final project!

CHAPTER 13

Scratch Projects Across the Curriculum

Due to its versatility and open ended format, Scratch is a tool that can be used across the curriculum in virtually every subject area. Once students understand the basic function of the coding blocks, they can use their creativity to display their content knowledge in a variety of ways. Scratch can be used in place of the traditional book report, three-sided science display, or math worksheet. How much fun could students have in preparing for a test when they could review by playing Scratch games created by their classmates!

Literacy Projects

Coding can play an integral part in helping students visualize the characters and settings they read about, as well as bring to life personal narratives they author themselves. The following literacy projects introduce young coders to some simple blocks that scaffold in understanding as the students progress in their knowledge and application of computational thinking skills.

The projects outlined here have been tested in the classroom and will continue to be updated on **Nofearcoding.org** based on teacher feedback. The lessons are built with the STRETCh philosophy and have been differentiated for struggling and advanced learners; however, you will note that the rubric is the same for all students. Criteria for mastery are in the center of the rubric, with room for teachers to write in comments for areas of struggle or extended thinking.

(Literacy) Hello Grandma and Grandpa

This project is designed for kindergarten students or early coders. The focus of the project is the Common Core State Standard of writing to narrate a single event and to provide a reaction to what happened. When creating the reaction, students will have their "Sprite" or character move toward the heart. This is a concrete, physical motion students can watch their character complete. When the student's sprite gets too close to the heart, they can simply drag their sprite back to its original location.

TABLE 13.1. Hello Grandma and Grandpa Literacy Project

GRADE	SCRATCH BLOCKS INTRODUCED	STANDARDS ADDRESSED
Kindergarten	move 10 steps	**ELA-Literacy.W.K.3:** Use a combination of drawing, dictating, and writing to narrate a single event or several loosely linked events, tell about the events in the order in which they occurred, and provide a reaction to what happened.
	say Hello! for 2 secs	

Students will use the "say" block to write what they would like to say. The differentiated No Fear Coding lesson uses a sentence frame for struggling writers, as well as extending the learning for those students who are ready to incorporate the cause and effect of motion. Access this project at **scratch.mit.edu/projects/129380641/**.

(Literacy) The Three Pigs Project

The Three Pigs Project is based on the popular children's story. The focus is on the first grade Common Core State Standard of Writing in which students recount two or more appropriately sequenced events. The Scratch blocks introduced in first grade will build on the knowledge of motion.

In kindergarten, students produced a reaction by making a Sprite move. In this project, they will make the pig move by gliding from one location to another. While *x* and *y* coordinates are used to make the pig glide, the project will already have these coordinates set for students. Access the project at **scratch.mit.edu/projects/129381230/.**

TABLE 13.2. Three Little Pigs Literacy Project

GRADE	SCRATCH BLOCKS INTRODUCED	STANDARDS ADDRESSED
First grade	wait **3** secs switch costume to Hay ▼ glide **1** secs to x: **0** y: **0**	**ELA-Literacy.W.1.3:** Write narratives in which they recount two or more appropriately sequenced events, include some details regarding what happened, use temporal words to signal event order, and provide some sense of closure.

Along with the writing standards, this project also incorporates the Common Core State Standard SL1.5, Speaking and Listening, which states, "add drawings or other visual displays to descriptions when appropriate to clarify ideas, thoughts and feeling." After reading or listening to story of the three little pigs, students will create their narrative using temporal words to signal events on paper. Then they will use their written dialogue to create their own Scratch project.

  ## Underwater Adventure

In this Scratch project, students will create a narrative using at least four characters. The focus should be on the order of events within the story and using transition words (time order words) for fluency and readability. Since every story will be different, this is a great activity to model the writing process for students by working through the student worksheets and creating a class story first. This will help support students who may struggling with writing, as you will be modeling the meta-cognitive process with everyone and they will come away with some story ideas from the whole group session.

While the main focus of this activity is the Common Core State Standard for Writing, there are many other second grade CCSS that can be addressed within this project. Access this project at **scratch.mit.edu/projects/127124642/.**

TABLE 13.3. Underwater Adventure Project

GRADE	SCRATCH BLOCKS INTRODUCED	STANDARDS ADDRESSED
Second grade	think Hmm... think Hmm... for 2 secs	**ELA-Literacy.W.2.3:** Write narratives in which they recount a well-elaborated event or short sequence of events, include details to describe actions, thoughts, and feelings, use temporal words to signal event order, and provide a sense of closure. **ELA-Literacy.L.2.1.E:** Use adjectives and adverbs, and choose between them depending on what is to be modified.
	repeat 10 move 10 steps	**ELA-Literacy.L.2.2:** Demonstrate command of the conventions of standard English capitalization, punctuation, and spelling when writing. **Math.Content.2.OA.A.1:** Use addition and subtraction within 100 to solve one- and two-step word problems involving situations of adding to, taking from, putting together, taking apart, and comparing, with unknowns in all positions.

Allow students who are more familiar with programming and or who finish quickly to explore movement of their characters. Students will build upon their knowledge of "move" and "glide," to include loops ("repeat") so that motion can be repeated in a more efficient ways.

Underwater Adventure will also have the students exploring concepts of time and cause and effect. Students' ability to use algorithms and procedures will grow by leaps and bounds as their stories come to life through dialogue and action.

As students become proficient with coding and computational thinking, these next three projects could be reviewed and revised each year. The Common Core State

Standards in Literacy focuses on Writing as a *process*. Once an author composes a draft, the piece of work then goes to a team for review. After review and feedback, changes are made and the process begins again. Much like the computational thinking practices listed below, coders will create multiple rough drafts.

Experimenting and iterating: Developing a little bit, then trying it out, then developing a bit more

Testing and debugging: Making sure things work and finding and solving problems when they arise

For this reason, the next three projects will introduce continue to build upon the previous use of Scratch blocks. It is recommended that the project itself should be reviewed, revised and built upon each year. Can you imagine the quality projects you will receive from students as they have worked on them for three years; receiving feedback and revising multiple times before publishing their final version their fifth grade year.

You will also notice in the chart that introduces the Scratch blocks and the Writing Project that there are Common Core State Standards in Writing and Reading Literature identified. This is to provide the classroom teacher the option of having students create their own original narratives, or elaborating on the characters and events from a literature based story. These lessons could also be easily adapted to non-fiction setting as well.

 Try it! Adapt one of the case study lessons modeled here to a classroom standard of your choosing. Share on the **Nofearcoding.org** website in the lesson gallery.

 Literacy

Choose Your Own Adventure

The purpose of this project is to plan and create a Scratch project that narrates a story with alternate endings or paths throughout.

Start the project by reviewing the *Choose Your Own Adventure* books based upon the concept created in 1976 by Edward Packard. These books were one of the most popular children's series during the 1980s and 90s, selling more than 250 million copies.

TABLE 12.4. Choose Your Own Adventure Project

GRADE	SCRATCH BLOCKS INTRODUCED	STANDARDS ADDRESSED
Third grade	ask What's your name? and wait go to mouse-pointer	**ELA-Literacy.W.3.3:** Write narratives to develop real or imagined experiences or events using effective technique, descriptive details, and clear event sequences. **ELA-Literacy.RL.3.3:** Describe characters in a story (e.g., their traits, motivations, or feelings) and explain how their actions contribute to the sequence of events
Fourth grade	when clicked forever switch costume to costume1 wait 1 secs switch costume to costume2 wait 1 secs when I receive conversation broadcast conversation and wait	**ELA-Literacy.W.4.3.B:** Use dialogue and description to develop experiences and events or show the responses of characters to situations. **ELA-Literacy.RL.4.3:** Describe in depth a character, setting, or event in a story or drama, drawing on specific details in the text (e.g., a character's thoughts, words, or actions).
Fifth grade	join hello answer	**ELA-Literacy.W.5.3.B:** Use narrative techniques, such as dialogue, description, and pacing, to develop experiences and events or show the responses of characters to situations. **ELA-Literacy.RL.5.3:** Compare and contrast two or more characters, settings, or events in a story or drama, drawing on specific details in the text (e.g., how characters interact).

Other standards covered by this project include:

ELA-Literacy.Y.W.3.3.A: Establish a situation and introduce a narrator and/or characters; organize an event sequence that unfolds naturally.

ELA-Literacy.W.3.3.B: Use dialogue and descriptions of actions, thoughts, and feelings to develop experiences and events or show the response of characters to situations.

ELA-Literacy.W.3.3.C: Use temporal words and phrases to signal event order.

ELA-Literacy.W.3.3.D: Provide a sense of closure.

ELA-Literacy.W.3.5: With guidance and support from peers and adults, develop and strengthen writing as needed by planning, revising, and editing.

When creating their own adventure, students will get to select from a variety of setting backdrops and can even create their own. Creativity can soar when combining coding within the curriculum!

Math projects

Scratch is a way for students to see math in action and for students to produce creative content about math. The Scratch game The Daily Life of Shapes was created by a 5th grade student who wanted to provide her little sister with a fun and engaging game for her sister to review her basic shapes.

Teachers can also use Scratch to explore mathematical concepts in action. "Go Bananas" takes an in-depth look at estimation. It is difficult to ascertain if a child can truly estimate when they are asked to do so on a worksheet. Who is to say they didn't actually count the objects?

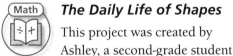 **The Daily Life of Shapes**

This project was created by Ashley, a second-grade student who created an interactive story game for her little sister to use to review shapes (Figure 13.2).

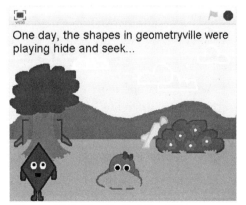

One day, the shapes in geometryville were playing hide and seek...

Figure 13.2. The Daily Life of Shapes, a student-created Scratch game.

The user of this game would be working on Common Core State Standard K.G.A.3, the Kindergarten Geometry standard that states "Identify and describe shapes (squares, circles, triangles, rectangles, hexagons, cubes, cones, cylinders, and spheres." The creator of the game used the skills learned from previously taught literacy projects, with the addition of the "broadcast," "receive," and "go to mouse-pointer" buttons. This project can be found at: **scratch.mit.edu/projects/146275252/**

TABLE 13.5. The Daily Life of Shapes Math Project

GRADE	SCRATCH BLOCKS INTRODUCED	STANDARDS ADDRESSED
Kindergarten	go to mouse-pointer when I receive conversation broadcast conversation and wait	**Math.Content.2.G.A.1:** Recognize and draw shapes having specified attributes, such as a given number of angles or a given number of equal faces. Identify triangles, quadrilaterals, pentagons, hexagons and cubes.

Go Bananas

Math

Estimation can be a hard concept for students to truly grasp. This is an abstract skill that can be made concrete in a number of ways. Fill a jar up with buttons, gumballs, almost any item and let students try to guess how many are in the jar. This is estimation that they can see, feel, and count.

When we try and move estimation to the representational level, it becomes a bit more difficult. In the Scratch game Go Bananas (Figure 13.3), students are asked to estimate the number of bunches of bananas they see on the screen before they disappear. Students will first play the game to check their estimation skills. The game will not give them enough time to physically count the bananas; they will be forced to estimate. Then, they will dive into the programming of Scratch to see how to change the values within the estimation game to recreate the game using their own values. The game can be found at: **scratch.mit.edu/projects/3185762/**

Figure 13.3. Go Bananas Scratch game for teaching estimation.

TABLE 13.6. Go Bananas Math Project

GRADE	SCRATCH BLOCKS INTRODUCED	STANDARDS ADDRESSED
Fourth grade	stamp pick random 1 to 10	**Math.Content.4.OA.A.3:** Solve multistep word problems posed with whole numbers and having whole-number answers using the four operations, including problems in which remainders must be interpreted. Represent these problems using equations with a letter standing for the unknown quantity. Assess the reasonableness of answers using mental computation and estimation strategies including rounding.

Science & Social Studies Projects

Science and social studies lend themselves to an open-ended, inquiry based learning experience. Scratch is a natural extension in allowing creativity and computational thinking to be visible inside of the content knowledge students are making connections with. When islands can talk and game review for test taking are used, engagement is increased.

Third Grade Island Project

Looking to change things up in Social Studies class this year? You can incorporate computational thinking by allowing students to substitute Scratch and coding for the traditional slide presentation.

While her classmates were required to create a poster of their islands, this third grade student approached her teacher and asked if she could code her project instead. She started with an image of the island of Sir Lanka, colored in the island, gave it a pair of glasses and created an animated mouth to make it talk (Figure 13.4).

Her coding blocks consisted of "switch backdrop to" so that she could switch the images from one to another, just like slides move from one to the next using PowerPoint or Google Slides. She even used her own voice and did a voice-over "recording" of the facts to make her poster come to life. With a few simple coding blocks, this third grader awed her teacher and her classmates!

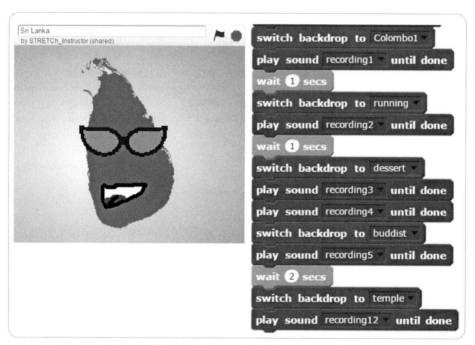

Figure 13.4. Animated Scratch "poster" third grade social studies project.

Magnetism and Electricity Project

More schools are making it mandatory that teachers pre-assess their students for prior knowledge at the beginning of each unit. Luckily for one fourth grader named Bailey, her teacher believed in differentiation and meeting the needs of all her students. Bailey had taken a pre-assessment on magnetism and electricity and scored an 88%. Rather than have the student sit through instruction that she had already mastered, the classroom teacher allowed the student to do an open-ended project.

Bailey decided to create a test review for her classmates using Scratch. The game-like environment had her hooked as she enjoyed solving puzzles and stretching her computational thinking skills. The teacher provided her with a copy of the test and she was off and coding for the next two weeks.

Using the "ask and wait" block, along with the "if <answer = yes> then" block, she created a game review of questions to help her classmates study. She also had inter-active exercises in which students had to use the arrow keys to move electrical wires to the correct location on a battery to make a lightbulb light up.

She even added a variable called "score," so that her classmates knew how many questions they got correct while studying. She decided to challenge the other fourth grade class and teacher by having her class use the game review for the test, while the other class would use the traditional Jeopardy Game Review that the teacher had created.

Upon completion of her project, the students in Bailey's class played the game and provided her with feedback. Many students pointed out that she needed to provide more time for students to read the verbal script, as they stated "they could barely read them." She was thrilled when students in her class outscored the other fourth grade classroom. Her class had 25 A's with the lowest test score being a 70%. The other classroom had four students who scored below a 50%. You can watch her YouTube video interview on the project at: **youtube.com/watch?v=QyWfNPpTNak**

Assessment for Scratch Projects

Another aspect that makes Scratch so appealing are the tools that can be used in conjunction with student work that can make their computational thinking visible. One such tool is Dr. Scratch (**drscratch.org**). This free web tool analyzes Scratch projects and gives feedback to educators and learners by assigning a computational thinking score to the projects. The score ranges from 0 to 21 points and is based on the degree of development in the areas of problem decomposition, logical thinking, synchronization, parallelism, algorithmic notions of flow control, user interactivity, and data representation. Dr. Scratch is a great tool for getting (and giving) feedback on projects. It even allows you to download a project certificate to share with students to encourage their progress (Figure 13.5).

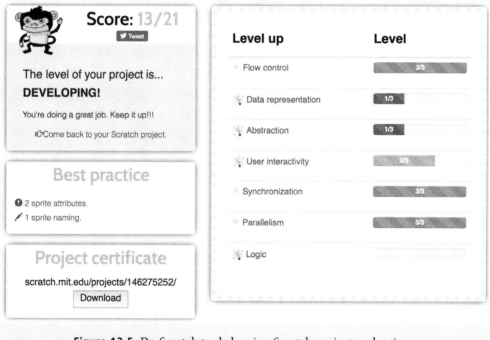

Figure 13.5. Dr. Scratch tool showing Scratch project evaluation.

Coding and Beyond

This final section looks ahead to cutting-edge technologies and experiences that may figure strongly in K–5 students' future. Location-based games and augmented reality are among the latest trends in educational technology. Players experience a hybrid world of virtual characters and media in physical space. This section explores some of the newest applications of augmented reality in the classroom. You will learn:

- Why teachers should use augmented reality to engage students and communities in real-world learning experiences.
- How to create a neighborhood tour in ARIS.
- What a walking tour of your community using ARIS looks like.

Create Real-World Experiences with ARIS

The augmented reality (AR) technology that captivated the world with Pokemon Go is already in use throughout classrooms. The University of Wisconsin, Madison created a free, open-source AR platform called ARIS (Augmented Reality for Interactive Storytelling). Using this technology, schools can create any number of immersive experiences for themselves and their communities. Bringing history and stories to life, building AR around current events, or helping students become engaged with their community—the possibilities are endless.

People all around the world use ARIS for variety of purposes. Most are involved with learning, from classrooms to museums, after school clubs, and community action. Elementary teachers can easily incorporate this form of coding and computational thinking into social studies and literacy standards through a community based tour.

One of the first ARIS projects was *Dow Day*, an interactive, location-based documentary for prospective students visiting the University of Wisconsin campus. The documentary was designed to allow future learners to experience a historic Madison protest that took place during the Vietnam War. The user was given the role of a reporter who was asked to cover a historic protest at the university in 1967 against the Dow Chemical Company. Jim Matthews, educational director of the Field Day Lab at UW Madison, shares the inspiration for the project.

> Students often think of history as events that happened somewhere else. I wanted to spark their curiosity about the history of their own community. After playing *Dow Day*, it is not uncommon for students to say things like, "Wow, I walk on Bascom Hill all the time and I never knew something like that happened here." Part of what grabs them is they can relate to the people, issues, and places in the story. After playing *Dow Day*, many folks are eager to create their own documentaries and stories. This opens up some great opportunities for community-based learning. (University of Wisconsin-Madison, 2012)

Figure 14.1. User perspective of *Dow Day*

While standing at the top of the hill on campus, the reporter sees video footage from when the students began to protest the Dow Chemical Corporation for making napalm for the war. As the reporter, you are sent on various quests to investigate the different interests and perspectives of students, police and Dow employees.

Why Teach with ARIS

No Fear Coding Mindset

By incorporating coding and computational thinking into your curriculum you have taken one step as an early adopter. You have also exercised your ability and the ability of your students to "live in beta," to troubleshoot, test, and find the answers to problems. Exploring the learning opportunities for emerging technologies is another way to proactively teach in the 21st century. To prepare students for the requirements of their future workplace, exposure to those tools and environments they will encounter is essential. Computer science is a growing field and many of today's students will be the creators of technologies such as ARIS.

Design Thinking

ARIS founder Jim Matthews shares that creating *Dow Day* required an "iterative process of research, design, and media production was required to translate source materials, such as photos of protest fliers or interviews from newspapers, into an interactive experience" (Univeristy of Wisconsin-Madison, 2012). Creating real-world scenarios and interactive stories requires the stages of design thinking. Students must have empathy for the user and consider their experience as they design the game. They must define their objectives and generate ideas for communicating them in a geographical situation. Finally, students will need to prototype and testing the experience to arrive at a finished project that others can use.

Community-Based Learning

Using augmented reality can connect users more deeply with their real surroundings (Krosinsky, 2011), and can be a powerful tool for the teacher looking to impart learning on the next field trip or excursion. It is also an innovative and interactive way to teach local or regional history, as it redefines the learning space of the traditional classroom. At the end of this chapter, you will hear from two educators who created a walking tour of their community in ARIS, and engaged their students and community in the process.

Deeper Connection with Subject Matter

Social studies teachers Beth Stofflet and Larry Moberly used ARIS during a unit on the African continent. Students were asked to choose from a list of social issues and then imagine a real person facing that issue. They used ARIS to tell interactive stories from that person's perspective (Medium, 2016).

How to Teach with ARIS

ARIS consists of three pieces of software

1. Client (app)—Used to play games and collect data

2. Editor—Interface used to make ARIS experiences

3. Server—Where games live on a database in the cloud. The client and editor read from and write to it. Upside: no need to install games or go through the app store. Downside: you need an internet connection to play.

Getting Started

To download the app visit **itunes.apple.com/us/app/aris/id371788434?mt=8** or search the iTunes store for ARIS. Once you have downloaded the app you'll need to create an account and login. Each player using ARIS needs an account.

The ARIS website has many manuals (**http://manual.arisgames.org/**) to help you get started. You will want to start with a basic understanding of objects, triggers, and scenes.

OBJECTS

Objects are containers for content you want your players to see or interact with. There are many types of objects, but think of each one as a type of media. When you work on class projects, each individual student's paper, video or picture would be considered one object.

TRIGGERS

In ARIS, the trigger is what connects the game world to the physical world. Think of a trigger something that will allow you to see the student paper, video or picture. For example, if you are going to visit a museum and you have your student draw a picture of the museum (the picture would be the object), you would place a trigger on the ARIS map at the location of the museum to trigger (an action) the picture to pop up on the screen as you walk up to the museum.

SCENES

Every game needs at least one scene to move action along. Every experience you are creating for your user must be within a scene, as it has to happen somewhere. For K-5 teachers just starting out, one scene for your game works well.

For the K-5 teacher, I would recommend starting out with the ARIS Basics course (**fielddaylab.org/courses/aris**). This will get you up and running with the basics of ARIS and using the objects, triggers, and scenes mentioned above. Be forewarned, you will need a laptop or desktop computer and an iPod or iPad for the ARIS app to get started. One downside of the APP is that it is currently only available for Apple products. There are plans of releasing and Android APP in the future.

Your next step would be to create a community tour using the ARIS website Mobile Tour Course (**fielddaylab.wisc.edu/courses/aris-neighborhood- tour**). In this course, educational director Jim Matthews introduces a basic design process that you will be able to use for this and future projects. The course takes about four hours to complete and is divided into nine lessons, but is well worth the investment of time.

The Community Tour

While many of the applications of ARIS have been for the middle and high school level, there is one application that K–5 teachers have been implementing in their classroom, the neighborhood tour.

Create a tour using ARIS that other people can play in order to learn more about your community and what it is like living there. Following are some elements of an engaging tour:

- It has a clear opening or introduction.
- It has a clear and consistent theme.
- It includes your personal perspective. The tour is written in *your* own voice or style and lets players into *your* world.
- It feels like it was made by an insider or someone with local knowledge.
- The conversations feel believable or realistic.
- It is well paced. It is not too long or too short and does not lag at certain points.
- Players are clear about what they need to do next throughout the tour.

Explore! Download ARIS and familiarize yourself with it by playing games that are currently being created by others around the world. Look for ways to connect your students with their community or create real-world experiences around content you are teaching.

Case Study—Walking Tour of Waukesha

Teachers are always looking for ways to engage students in a project based learning environment. Traci Koepke and Tiffany Humphrey, two third grade teachers from Waukesha, Wisconsin, decided to take their social studies unit on Waukesha history to the next level using ARIS. A description of their journey follows.

We are fortunate to be able to team teach a class of 43 third graders. Our team had an upcoming social studies activity that encompassed learning about our town's history. In previous years this activity involved students getting on a bus and riding around the town while their teacher read facts about the history of the city. We were looking for a way to have our students do that "heavy lifting" by learning about the history of our town and sharing their research with the community.

With the pressure of needing to meet all the standards, we knew that we had to look at this unit with a different lens. We began with the end in mind by looking at the required standards. Next, we brainstormed a list of infrastructures that make our city successful (Figure 14.2). After many drafts and discussions, we crafted our essential question: "What historical events/infrastructures contributed to the success of our city?"

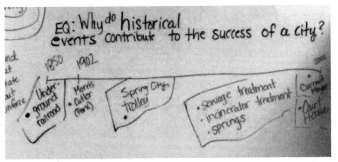

Figure 14.2. Brainstorming board for Waukesha history project.

The team wanted to work smarter, not harder, so we looked at which reading, writing, and speaking standards could also be incorporated into this unit. On note cards, the standards were written in "I Can Statements" that would ultimately be proven by student evidence.

The conversation then turned to how students would show their evidence of learning for each standard. We decided to create a research guide that would help students organize their thinking. For example, one statement read, "I can identify the important infrastructures that help the city be successful." In small groups, students would create a graphic organizer on their device listing all the infrastructures they could think of.

Then students met to share out their thinking and a class web was created. Students would sit in a circle and use their conversational moves during the discussion. For example, Christy and Mike said, "I think one of the important infrastructures of our city is transportation. Another group responded by saying, "I would have to agree with what they said. We also added the airport to our web which goes with transportation." Below is an example of a student web that was copied and pasted into the research book.

Students created a list of two infrastructures that they were interested in diving deeper into. Our team looked at the student lists and created student partnerships. The partnerships began researching using a variety of books and internet resources. In the research guide, students began answering the following questions: Where, when and what.

The end result for our students was to create a flyer to share their research about their infrastructure. After about a week in a half of our students researching, many of our groups were ready to begin the writing process of their flyer. During this time, we were able to incorporate many of our nonfiction writing standards and conventions. To the right, you will see an example of a flyer. Students also needed to include a question at the end of the flyer for the reader to respond to.

After all of the flyers were completed, another social studies standard that was incorporated was "I can determine the time and sequence of a historical event." As a class, students had to figure out when their infrastructure fell on the timeline. The conversations that occurred during this time were amazing! It is very useful to have a tack strip available so students can easily move their flyer around.

One example of a rubric that we used for this standard also incorporated depth of knowledge (DOK) levels (Figure 14.3). This information was shared with the students before they began to write their flyer. When we met with the students after their flyer was complete, we had the students self-evaluate themselves using this rubric. Then we evaluated them using the rubric and provided students with feedback.

Name

Date

Goal: I can determine the time, sequence, and cause/effect of a historical event. (RI 3)

4	3	2	1
Investigate and draw conclusions about how your event impacts the world today (DOK 4)	How is your event related to the success of the city (DOK 3)	What logical predication can you make about your event (DOK 2)	Where did you place your event on the timeline? (DOK 1)

Figure 14.3. DOK rubric used in activity.

The next step was integrating the flyers into ARIS. Our team copied and paste the flyers into the app to prepare for our field trip. On the day of the field trip, students were in small groups with a parent volunteer. We used one device for two students. Students would then either hotspot off a volunteer's phone or a portable hotspot unit. We also created parent tour guides. In the book, parents could see approximately where they triggers were located and how many there were. These images were screen shot directly from the ARIS app. Here is an example of one of our stops. We have found that four stops for a field from from 9:00-2:00 seems to be a manageable amount for our third graders.

When we arrived at a location in our community, there were approximately 4-5 triggers in a given area. This gave student groups the opportunity to spread out and learn about an infrastructure that their peer researched. Student partnerships took turns reading the flyer to each other that popped up. Then they would respond to the question at the end of the flyer and record their thinking in the notebook located inside ARIS.

ARIS took our classes learning to the next step from passive learning to active learning. Students were able to dig right into the research and share the facts with the class and the community. One students said, "This is awesome! I am learning from my friends and about my community!"

Conclusion

Coding and computational thinking are essential 21st century learning skills that should have been implemented almost twenty years ago. Our educational system is moving at a snail's pace and we need to get more educators on board with the use of technology to change thinking.

Advances in neuroscience have had a great impact upon how scientists and educators view learning. Rather than being the sage on the stage and imparting our knowledge onto thy students, we must turn our role into the meddler in the middle. Learning alongside our students and empowering their abilities to think computationally will build our global community into a more productive and self-sustaining world.

By reading this book and putting the aptitudes and skills into practice, educators will help K–5 students move from the concrete to the representational to the abstract in their understanding of how computers can help humans become more efficient in their ability to process and make sense of information. From the Bee-Bot to Code.org resources to the open-ended projects created in Scratch, student creativity and content knowledge can be infused with coding skills.

The final concluding statements of this book come from two students with very different vantage points—a middle school student who began using Scratch in third grade and has been passionate about spreading the word to others, and a student in a teacher education program who sees the benefits coding and computational thinking have for educators.

Student Perspective—Bailey Williams

In the setting of a daily classroom, many lessons are taught and progressively learned throughout the day; whether it comes to history, math, science, or any other subject of the sort. The basics of teaching these lessons are mostly textbooks being read and information being recited, but many don't know that more can be absorbed from hands-on experience such as computer programming and Scratch.

During my third-grade year of elementary school, my class did individual projects based on their own selection of a non-American island and its culture. Instead of going the normal route and doing a physical presentation of my island, Sri Lanka, I decided to make a Scratch project that functioned like a presentation instead. My fellow students and teachers were impressed by the demonstration and some tried Scratch themselves. The following year another opportunity presented itself to engage my peers in Scratch yet again, this time to help them in a review of electro-magnetism for the unit test. The Scratch game I created was a highly interactive simulation that allowed the students to input their name, answer questions and physically connect components of a battery that would help them in preparation for the test. When the results of my classes' overall grade on the test came through almost more than three quarters of them had gotten at least an A-.

In my experience the availability of Scratch and other early programming sites is crucial to the new era of students, mainly because of the multiple benefits that will come of it in the future of new technology, as well as the benefits that it will present in the current setting in the classroom.

Future Educator Perspective—Ashley Kitzerow

As a current student and future educator, I have had limited experience with coding in the classroom. I was introduced to Scratch my freshman year of high school, and that was my first experience with coding. Unfortunately, my grade school district did not have any coding incorporated into their curriculum. However, after I was introduced to Scratch, I found myself looking for ways I could incorporate it into my educational career so that my peers and teachers could see the benefits of using coding in the classroom. The classes in which I found these opportunities were the ones in which the teacher had a project-based curriculum.

The first opportunity I had to use Scratch as a student was not until my sophomore year of high school during my German class. We had to create a project which showed we understood the terminology and etiquette used in restaurants in Germany. I used Scratch to create a short video simulating somebody ordering food at a restaurant, to show I had mastered the skills and vocabulary from the unit. Many of my peers simply worked in groups and acted out ordering food at a restaurant. While they still were able to show their skill mastery through skits, I benefited from being allowed to use Scratch because I prefer to work alone on projects rather than in groups. There are many other students who would benefit from Scratch simply because it allows them to show mastery of skills that would otherwise require a group effort. While I was in high school, this was the main benefit I saw from

131

coding. However, once I got to college and began to look at coding from an educator's perspective I began to notice more benefits that I hadn't noticed before.

Since starting college, I have only had one opportunity to use coding, and; unfortunately, it wasn't a part of any curriculum. For one of my English courses, I completed an H-Options project (an additional project designed by the student so they can receive honors credit for a course that is not honors) and was able to use Scratch as part of the project. After reading am Iroquois creation story (a story explaining how the Iroquois believe the world was created), I recreated the story using Scratch and then designed a lesson plan. In this lesson, I had the students each use Scratch to recreate the story, with the lesson objective being the understanding that the replication of the exact same message cannot be sent using multiple mediums. Meaning that it is impossible to *exactly* recreate the Iroquois Creation story they read using Scratch because there are some textual ideas that cannot be represented with moving pictures.

Technology is an integral part of today's society, but it is often left untaught in schools because the teachers know less about technology than the students do. Through this project, I developed the belief that this common myth is untrue. There is much about technology that children do not know, and if our educators are willing to take the time to educate themselves on topics such as coding, they can open a whole new world through which students can learn. By using coding, an educator can not only spark students' future interest to go into technological fields of work, but it also allows teachers to reach students they may have been unable to reach before. Coding is a very logical process, and for those who are logical thinkers, using Scratch may allow them to comprehend a topic that was confusing to them before.

Something else I learned through this project was that students using coding forces them to develop a deep understanding of the concept they are learning about. By using coding programs such as Scratch, the student must slow down their thinking and break the concept down into smaller chunks. For example, when I was recreating the Iroquois Creation story, I had to go over the story sentence by sentence and ask myself, "Can this be shown using pictures?" Through this process, I developed a much more thorough understanding of the story than I had before. As educators one goal to keep in mind is to have the students develop a deep, not surface, understanding of the curriculum. Using coding is one way this can be done. By having students develop a deep understanding of the curriculum, the teacher is also setting them up to be successful critical thinkers, which is a useful tool to have as a student and citizen.

References

Barr, D., Harrison, J., & Conery, L. (2011). Computational Thinking: A Digital Age Skill for Everyone. Retrieved from https://www.iste.org/docs/learning-and-leading-docs/march-2011-computational-thinking-ll386.pdf

Barr, V., & Stephenson, C. (2011). Bringing computational thinking to K–12. *ACM Inroads, 2*(1), 48-54.

Boaler, J., & Dweck, C. (2016). *Mathematical mindsets: unleashing students' potential through creative math, inspiring messages, and innovative teaching.* San Francisco, CA: Jossey-Bass.

Brennan, K., & Resnick, M. (2012). Using artifact-based interviews to study the development of computational thinking in interactive media design. [Paper presented at annual American Educational Research Association meeting, Vancouver, BC, Canada] Retrieved from http://scratched.gse.harvard.edu/ct/files/AERA2012.pdf

Code.org. (n.d.). Making Computer Science Fundamental to K–12 Education. Retrieved from https://code.org/files/Making_CS_Fundamental.pdf

Computational Thinking | Defining. (n.d.). Retrieved February 20, 2017, from http://scratched.gse.harvard.edu/ct/defining.html

Computer Science Teachers Association & Association for Computing Machinery. (n.d.). *Bugs in the System: Computer Science Teacher Certification in the US.* Retrieved from http://c.ymcdn.com/sites/www.csteachers.org/resource/resmgr/CSTA_BugsInTheSystem.pdf?hhSearchTerms="bugs+and+system"

Cuny, J., Snyder, L., & Wing, J.M. (2010). Demystifying computational thinking for non-computer scientists. Retrieved from http://www.cs.cmu.edu/~CompThink/resources/TheLinkWing.pdf

Dasgupta, S., Hale, W., Monroy-Hernandez, A., & Mako Hil, B. (n.d.). Remixing as a Pathway to Computational Thinking. Retrieved from https://www.microsoft.com/en-us/research/wp-content/uploads/2016/02/remixing.pdf

Common Core State Standards Initiative. (2017). English Language Arts Standards » Anchor Standards » College and Career Readiness Anchor Standards for Reading. (n.d.). Retrieved from http://www.corestandards.org/ELA-Literacy/CCRA/R/

Everette, M. (n.d.). A Guide to the 8 Mathematical Practice Standards [Web log post]. Retrieved from https://www.scholastic.com/teachers/blog-posts/meghan-everette/guide-8-mathematical-practice-standards/

New Media Institute. (2014). Game-Based Learning: What It Is, Why It Works, And Where It's Going. Retrieved from http://www.lessonpaths.com/learn/i/game-based-learning-in-the-elementary-classroom/gamebased-learning-what-it-is-why-it-works-and-where-its-going

Google. (n.d.). Google for Education: Computational Thinking. Retrieved March 05, 2017, from https://edu.google.com/resources/programs/exploring-computational-thinking/index.html#!ct-overview

Grover, S., & Pea, R. (2013). Computational thinking in K–12: A review of the state of the field. *Educational Researcher, 42*(1), 38-43.

Guzdial, M. (2008). Education: Paving the way for computational thinking. *Communications of the ACM, 51*(8), 25-27. doi: 10.1145/1378704.1378713

International Society for Technology in Education & Computer Science Teachers Association. (2011). *Operational Definition of Computational Thinking.* Retrieved from http://www.iste.org/docs/ct-documents/computational-thinking-operational-definition-flyer.pdf

Johnson, M. (2015). *Should My Kid Learn to Code?* [Web log post]. Retrieved from https://research.googleblog.com/2015/07/should-my-kid-learn-to-code_14.html

Kazemi, E., & Lomax, K. (2016). *Modeling with Mathematics.* Retrieved from https://www.teachingchannel.org/blog/2016/05/13/modeling-with-math-nsf/

Khan Academy. (2011). *Cylinder Volume and Surface Area.* Retrieved from https://www.youtube.com/watch?v=gL3HxBQyeg0

Krosinksy, S. (2011). *Augmented Reality Enhances Learning*. Retrieved from http://news.unm.edu/news/augmented-reality-enhances-learning.

Lee, I., Martin, F., Denner, J., Coulter, B., Allan, W., Erickson, J., Malyn-Smith, J., Werner, L. (2011). Computational thinking for youth in practice. *ACM Inroads, 2*(1), 32-37.

Logo History. (2015). Retrieved from http://el.media.mit.edu/logo-foundation/what_is_logo/history.html

McCallum, W., & Zimba, J. (2011). Retrieved from https://www.youtube.com/watch?v=m1rxkW8ucAI&list=PLD7F4C7DE7CB3D2E6

Meyer, D. (2010). Retrieved from https://www.ted.com/talks/dan_meyer_math_curriculum_makeover

Moreno-León, J., & Robles, G. (2016). Dr. Scratch: supporting teachers in the assessment of computational thinking. Retrieved from http://www.ictinpractice.com-dr-scratch-supporting-teachers-in-the-assessment-of-computational-thinking/

Moreno-León,, J., & Robles, G. (2015). Analyze your Scratch projects with Dr. Scratch and assess. Retrieved from http://jemole.me/replication/2015scratch/InferCT.pdf

MotivatingSuccess: Stuck on an Elevator - Take Action. [Video file]. (2012, May 16). Retrieved February 05, 2017, from https://www.youtube.com/watch?v=VrSUe_m19FY

NAFCareerAcads Follow. (2013, July 18). *ComputationalThinking: Why It is Important for All Students*. Retrieved from https://www.slideshare.net/NAFCareerAcads/computational-thinking-an-important-skill-for-all-students-naf-next-20132

National Research Council. (2010). Report of a workshop on the scope and nature of computational thinking. Washington, DC: National Academies Press.

National Research Council. (2011). Report of a workshop on the pedagogical aspects of computational thinking. Washington, DC: National Academies Press.

Norris, K. (2016). *Engage in the Mathematical Practices*. Bloomington, IN: Solution Tree Press.

Patterson, S. (2014). Coding for Kindergarteners. Retrieved from https://www.edutopia.org/blog/coding-for-kindergarteners-sam-patterson

Phillips, R., & Brooks, B. (January). *The Hour of Code: Impact on Attitudes Towards and Self-Efficacy with Computer Science*. Retrieved from https://code.org/files/HourOfCodeImpactStudy_Jan2017.pdf

Reinhart, S. (2000, April). Never Say Anything a Kid Can Say! *Mathematics Teaching in The Middle School, 5*(8), 54-57.

Repenning, A., Webb, D., & Ioannidou, A. (2010). *Scalable game design and the development of a checklist for getting computational thinking into public schools. Proceedings of the 41st ACM technical symposium on Computer science education* SIGCSE '10. doi:10.1145/1734263.1734357

Resnick M, Silverman B, Kafai Y, Maloney J, Monroy-Herna´ndez A, Rusk N et al. (2009) Scratch: programming for all. *Communications of the ACM 52*(11):60

Román-González, M., Moreno-León, J., & Robles, G. (2015, September). Dr. Scratch: Automatic Analysis of Scratch Projects to Assess and Foster Computational Thinking. Retrieved March 05, 2017, from https://www.researchgate.net/publication/281714025_Dr_Scratch_Automatic_Analysis_of_Scratch_Projects_to_Assess_and_Foster_Computational_Thinking

Shein, E. (2014). Should everybody learn to code? Commun. ACM, 57(2), 16-18. doi: 10.1145/2557447

Standards for Mathematical Practice. (n.d.). Retrieved February 26, 2017, from http://www.corestandards.org/Math/Practice/

Stephenson, C., Cooper, S., Owens, B. B., & Gal-Ezer, J. (2012). The new CSTA K-12 computer science standards. Proceedings of the 17th ACM annual conference on Innovation and technology in computer science education - ITiCSE '12. doi:10.1145/2325296.2325380

TEDTalks. (2013). *Living in beta: Molly Schroeder at TEDxBurnsvilleED* [Video file]. Retrieved from https://www.youtube.com/watch?v=0nnYI3ePrY8

TEDTalks. (2009). *Simon Sinek--How Great Leaders Inspire Action* [Video file]. Retrieved from https://www.ted.com/talks/simon_sinek_how_great_leaders_inspire_action

Prince EA. (2016, September 26). *The People vs. the School System*. [Video File]. Retrieved from https://www.youtube.com/watch?v=dqTTojTija8

Tinker RF, Xie Q. (2008). Applying computational science to education: the molecular workbench paradigm. *Computer Science Engineering 10*(5):24–27.

University of Wisconsin-Madison. (2012). *Examples of Situated Learning Genres.* Retrieved from http://engage.wisc.edu/sl/examples.html

Wagganer, E. L. (2015). Creating Math Talk Communities. *Teaching Children Mathematics,22*(4), 248.

Werrell, B. (2014). *Why Learning to Code Benefits Kids, Regardless of Future Career Choice.* Retrieved from http://blog.connectionsacademy.com/why-learning-to-code-benefits-kids-regardless-of-future-career-choice/

Code.org. (n.d.) *What's wrong with this picture?* Retrieved from https://code.org/promote.

Wing, J.M. (2006). Computational thinking. *Communications of the ACM, 49*(3), 33-35.

World Economic Forum. (2016). New Vision for Education: Fostering Social and Emotional Learning through Technology. Retrieved from http://www3.weforum.org/docs/WEF

Appendix A

ISTE Standards for Students

The ISTE Standards for Students emphasize the skills and qualities we want for students, enabling them to engage and thrive in a connected, digital world. The standards are designed for use by educators across the curriculum, with every age student, with a goal of cultivating these skills throughout a student's academic career. Both students and teachers will be responsible for achieving foundational technology skills to fully apply the standards. The reward, however, will be educators who skillfully mentor and inspire students to amplify learning with technology and challenge them to be agents of their own learning.

1. **Empowered Learner**

   Students leverage technology to take an active role in choosing, achieving and demonstrating competency in their learning goals, informed by the learning sciences. Students:

   a. articulate and set personal learning goals, develop strategies leveraging technology to achieve them and reflect on the learning process itself to improve learning outcomes.

   b. build networks and customize their learning environments in ways that support the learning process.

   c. use technology to seek feedback that informs and improves their practice and to demonstrate their learning in a variety of ways.

   d. understand the fundamental concepts of technology operations, demonstrate the ability to choose, use and troubleshoot current technologies and are able to transfer their knowledge to explore emerging technologies.

2. Digital Citizen

Students recognize the rights, responsibilities and opportunities of living, learning and working in an interconnected digital world, and they act and model in ways that are safe, legal and ethical. Students:

    a. cultivate and manage their digital identity and reputation and are aware of the permanence of their actions in the digital world.

    b. engage in positive, safe, legal and ethical behavior when using technology, including social interactions online or when using networked devices.

    c. demonstrate an understanding of and respect for the rights and obligations of using and sharing intellectual property.

    d. manage their personal data to maintain digital privacy and security and are aware of data-collection technology used to track their navigation online.

3. Knowledge Constructor

Students critically curate a variety of resources using digital tools to construct knowledge, produce creative artifacts and make meaningful learning experiences for themselves and others. Students:

    a. plan and employ effective research strategies to locate information and other resources for their intellectual or creative pursuits.

    b. evaluate the accuracy, perspective, credibility and relevance of information, media, data or other resources.

    c. curate information from digital resources using a variety of tools and methods to create collections of artifacts that demonstrate meaningful connections or conclusions.

    d. build knowledge by actively exploring real-world issues and problems, developing ideas and theories and pursuing answers and solutions.

4. Innovative Designer

Students use a variety of technologies within a design process to identify and solve problems by creating new, useful or imaginative solutions. Students:

    a. know and use a deliberate design process for generating ideas, testing theories, creating innovative artifacts or solving authentic problems.

    b. select and use digital tools to plan and manage a design process that considers design constraints and calculated risks.

    c. develop, test and refine prototypes as part of a cyclical design process.

    d. exhibit a tolerance for ambiguity, perseverance and the capacity to work with open-ended problems.

5. **Computational Thinker**

Students develop and employ strategies for understanding and solving problems in ways that leverage the power of technological methods to develop and test solutions. Students:

    a. formulate problem definitions suited for technology-assisted methods such as data analysis, abstract models and algorithmic thinking in exploring and finding solutions.

    b. collect data or identify relevant data sets, use digital tools to analyze them, and represent data in various ways to facilitate problem-solving and decision-making.

    c. break problems into component parts, extract key information, and develop descriptive models to understand complex systems or facilitate problem-solving.

    d. understand how automation works and use algorithmic thinking to develop a sequence of steps to create and test automated solutions.

6. **Creative Communicator**

Students communicate clearly and express themselves creatively for a variety of purposes using the platforms, tools, styles, formats and digital media appropriate to their goals. Students:

    a. choose the appropriate platforms and tools for meeting the desired objectives of their creation or communication.

    b. create original works or responsibly repurpose or remix digital resources into new creations.

    c. communicate complex ideas clearly and effectively by creating or using a variety of digital objects such as visualizations, models or simulations.

    d. publish or present content that customizes the message and medium for their intended audiences.

7. **Global Collaborator**
   Students use digital tools to broaden their perspectives and enrich their learning by collaborating with others and working effectively in teams locally and globally. Students:

   a. use digital tools to connect with learners from a variety of backgrounds and cultures, engaging with them in ways that broaden mutual understanding and learning.

   b. use collaborative technologies to work with others, including peers, experts or community members, to examine issues and problems from multiple viewpoints.

   c. contribute constructively to project teams, assuming various roles and responsibilities to work effectively toward a common goal.

   d. explore local and global issues and use collaborative technologies to work with others to investigate solutions.

Appendix B

Coding and the Standards for Mathematical Practice

This appendix will show how you can support coding through the application of computational thinking within the Common Core State Standard Mathematical Practices. Each standard will be mapped to the ISTE Standards for Students. Individual standards will also be broken down to show the connections to the ISTE and Computer Science Teacher Association's (CSTA) computational thinking vocabulary. Tables for each standard detail how K–5 students progress through the standards using computational thinking.

Standard 1

CCSS.Math.Practice.MP1: Make sense of problems and persevere in solving them.

ISTE Standards for Students: Computational Thinker 5b, 5c

You will find this mathematical practice standard in every math problem, every day. It means that students must first understand the problem, find an organized way to attack it, and work until it is done. Let's decompose the standard and see how it relates to computational thinking. Vocabulary that relates to computational thinking has been bolded in the following standard description.

*Mathematically proficient students start by explaining to themselves the **meaning of a problem** and looking for **entry points** to its solution. They **analyze givens, constraints, relationships and goals**. They make conjectures about the form and **meaning of the solution** and **plan a solution pathway** rather than simply jumping into a solution attempt. They **consider analogous problems**, and **try special cases** and **simpler forms** of the original problem in order to **gain insight into its solution**. They monitor and evaluate their progress and change course if necessary.*

*Mathematically proficient students **can explain correspondence between equations, verbal descriptions, tables, and graphs or draw diagrams of important features and relationships, graph data**, and **search for regularity or trends**. Younger students might rely on using concrete objects or pictures to help conceptualize and solve a problem.*

*Mathematically proficient students check their answers to problems using a different method, and they continually ask themselves, **"Does this make sense?"** They can identify correspondences between different approaches.*

ISTE/CSTA COMPUTATIONAL THINKING VOCABULARY

Abstraction: Meaning of a problem, meaning of a solution

Problem Decomposition: Entry points, plan a solution pathway

Data Collection: Analyze givens, constraints, relationships and goals

Data Analysis: Consider analogous problems, try special cases, simpler forms, gain insight into its solution, ask "Does this make sense?"

Data Representation: Explain correspondence between equations, verbal descriptions, tables, and graphs or draw diagrams of important features and relationships, graph data; search for regularity or trends

How to Teach It

Teachers should give students tough problems and wait them out. Allowing wait time for yourself and your students will be the toughest obstacle to overcome with this standard. Work for growth in thinking and the "aha" moments. Teachers will know they are on the right track when math becomes about the process and not about the one right answer. The key is to lead with questions and not with your chalk, pencil, or smartboard pen.

Begin by encouraging students to estimate a solution prior to starting the task. Ask questions and provide manipulatives. Manipulatives are not only for K–2 teachers. They should be used by all K–5 teachers as a way to allow for students to productively struggle without lowering the cognitive demand for the task. Then have students share solutions and strategies, while having them intentionally make connections.

K–5 Student Progression for Standard 1

Kindergarten	Students begin to build an understanding: "doing math" is actually solving a problem. They wrestle with the meaning of the problem by solving through trial and error.
First Grade	Students realize that "doing math" involves solving a problem. They begin to look for the meaning of the problem before they begin. They are beginning to identify critical information needed to solve problems.
Second Grade	Students look for meaning in the problem and will begin to plan out a problem solving approach. They can locate critical information needed to solve the problem. They are beginning to identify when they need to make changes in their solution pathways to arrive at a reasonable answer.
Grades 3–5	Students can provide a reasonable estimate prior to solving a problem. Students can identify when they need to make changes in their solution pathways to arrive at a reasonable answer. Students will look for meaning and listen to the strategies of others for meaning, as well as errors in thinking. They will try different approaches and look for the most efficient way to solve problems. At this point, students should be using another method to check and justify the validity of their answers.

Standard 2

CCSS.Math.Practice.MP2: Reason abstractly and quantitatively.

2016 ISTE Student Standard: Computational Thinker 5c

This is probably the hardest of standards for those without a mathematical degree. There is a reason why most elementary teachers do not major in mathematics. That said, this is one of the most important concepts for teachers and parents to understand. It boils down to making sure that student not only understand the standard algorithm for math, but also what the algorithm means.

*Mathematically proficient students make sense of quantities and their relationships in problem situations. They bring two complementary abilities to bear on problems involving quantitative relationships: the ability to decontextualize - to abstract a given situation and **represent it symbolically and manipulate the representing symbols as if they have a life of their own, without necessarily attending to their referents** —and the ability to contextualize—to pause as needed during the manipulation process in order to probe into the referents for the symbols involved. Quantitative reasoning entails habits of creating a coherent representation of the problem at hand; considering the units involved; attending to the meaning of quantities, not just how to compute them; and knowing the flexibility using different properties of operations and objects.*

ISTE/CSTA COMPUTATIONAL THINKING VOCABULARY

Abstraction: Represent it symbolically (with the written numeral '8') and manipulate the representing symbols as if they have a life of their own, without necessarily attending to their referents (referents = 8 physical objects).

How to Teach It

Having students draw representations of a problem, while working with the manipulatives will provide students with the means to figure out what to do with the data themselves. Allow students to move from the manipulatives (concrete) to symbolic drawings (representations), to the algorithms (abstract).

Young students progress with the knowledge that five objects equal the number five (5). From there they begin to use manipulatives and explore fact families. If fact families are only done with the abstract numbers the students never solidify their ability to reason abstractly. For students to truly understand the abstract, they must be able to apply the concepts to their referents (manipulatives) first. Teachers can help engage students in this mathematical practice by asking questions such as:

- What do you know about this problem?

- What do the numbers represent?

- What strategy have you used so far? (Can students identify if their strategy is concrete, representational or abstract?)

- How can you represent this situation with objects, drawings, numbers?

Just like reading uses the "read-aloud" to demonstrate teacher metacognitive thinking, teachers can use the "think-aloud" in math to demonstrated their own computational thinking in action.

K–5 Student Progression for Standard 2

Kindergarten	Students begin to recognize that numbers represent a specific quantity of something. They also connect the quantity to the written symbol.
First Grade	Students begin to compose and decompose quantities and construct written equations and fact families. For example: $4 + 5 = 9$ $5 + 4 = 9$ $9 - 5 = 4$ $9 - 4 = 5$
Second Grade	Students solidify understand and use properties of operations and can related addition and subtraction to the length of an object.
Third Grade	Students can connect quantity to written symbols. They use this knowledge to create a logical representation of problems, considering both the quantities and the units needed to represent those quantities.
Grades 4–5	Students understanding moves from whole numbers to fractions and decimals. Students can write simple expressions, record calculations with numbers, and represent or round numbers using place value concepts.

Standard 3

CCSS.Math.Practice.MP3: Construct viable arguments and critique the reasoning of others.

2016 ISTE Student Standard: Computational Thinker 5

It is important that students are able to talk about math using mathematical language to support or refute the work of others. Communication and Collaboration are two key 21st century skills that have been identified in a variety of content specific domains. If we want our students to acquire these skills, then we must intentionally model, teach and assess them on these skills.

*Mathematically proficient students understand and **use stated assumptions, defini-tions, and previously established results in constructing arguments**. They make conjectures and build a **logical progression of statements** to explore the truth of their conjectures. They are able to **analyze situations by breaking them into cases**, and can recognize and use counter examples. They **justify their conclusions, communicate them to others, and respond to the arguments of others**. They reason inductively about data, making plausible arguments that take into account the context from which the data arose.*

*Mathematically proficient students are also able to compare the effectiveness of two plausible argument, **distinguish correct logic or reasoning from that which is flawed**, and–if there is a flaw in argument–explain what it is. Elementary students can **construct arguments** using concrete referents such as objects, drawings, diagrams, and actions. Such arguments can make sense and be correct, even though they are not gen-eralized or made formal until later grades. Students at all grades can listen or read the arguments of others, decide whether they make sense, and ask useful questions to clarify or improve the arguments.*

ISTE/CSTA COMPUTATIONAL THINKING VOCABULARY

Data Analysis: Use stated assumptions, definitions, and previously established results in constructing arguments; distinguish correct logic or reasoning from that which is flawed;

Problem Decomposition: Able to analyze situations by breaking them into cases

Algorithms & Procedures: Logical progression of statements; construct arguments

Simulation: Justify their conclusions, communicate them to others, and respond to the arguments of others

How to Teach It

Teachers should post mathematical vocabulary and make students use it. Teacher practices have always included questioning, but students also need to be provided with sentence frames in order for students to understand the correct context with which to use these words.

K–5 Student Progression for Standard 3

Kindergarten	Students begin to develop mathematical communication skills by referring to objects and drawings and asking questions such as: How did you get that? Students also explain their own thinking and listen to the thinking of others, as well as respond back with the help of simple sentence frames.
Grades 1–2	Students expand their communication to include error analysis in identifying when someone's thinking may not be correct. They communicate their own thinking and ask questions to determine if others' explanations make sense. Students start asking: How did you get that? Explain your thinking. Why is that true?
Third Grade	Students work on refining their thinking, but should still be using concrete manipulatives and representational drawings to support their thinking. Students ask questions and are strengthening how they respond to others' thinking.
Grades 4–5	Students should be moving toward the use of standard algorithms to demonstrate their thinking; however still use correct verbal explanations that demonstrate cohesive quantitative reasoning. They should refine their thinking by understanding the strategies of others and be able to explain which strategy is best for them and why.

Standard 4

CCSS.Math.Practice.MP4: Model with mathematics.

2016 ISTE Student Standard: Computational Thinker 5c

Understanding the word around us is essential for adult success. Creating representations and models of processes is how we interact with our surroundings. Young children are continually taking input from their surroundings and trying to "make sense of it."

Mathematically proficient students **can apply the mathematics they know to solve problems arising in everyday life, society, and the workplace**. *In early grades, this might be as simple as writing an addition equation to describe a situation. In middle* *grades, a student might apply proportional reasoning to plan a school event or analyze a problem in the community...*

*Mathematically proficient students who can apply what they know are comfortable making assumptions and approximations to **simplify a complicated situation,** realizing that these may need revision later. They are able to identify important criteria in a practical situation and **map their relationships using such tools as diagrams, two-way tables, graphs, flowcharts and formulas**. They can analyze those relationships mathematically to draw conclusions. They routinely interpret their mathematical results in the context of the situation and reflect on whether the results make sense, possibly improving the model if it has not served its purpose.*

ISTE/CSTA COMPUTATIONAL THINKING VOCABULARY

Abstraction: Simplify a complicated situation

Automation: Map their relationships using such tools as diagrams, two-way tables, graphs, flowcharts and formulas

Simulation: Can apply the mathematics they know to solve problems arising in everyday life, society, and the workplace

How to Teach It

With the implementation of the reading workshop, K-5 teachers are familiar with the "Read Aloud," in which teachers model their metacognitive thinking so that students can see and hear what good readers do. Similarly with mathematics, teachers can model and connect different representations and processes that students can use to solve tasks by using a "Think Aloud."

K–5 Student Progression for Standard 4

Grades K–2	In grades K–2, students experiment with representing problems using objects, pictures, numbers, words, charts, lists and even acting the problem out. Students need time to create connections between the way in which they represent problems and how others represent problems. Allowing time for students to make their thinking visible and explain how they arrived at their answer will help them increase the strategies they can use. Students should be expected to use a variety of strategies
Grades 3–4	Students will expand upon their skills by evaluating the strategies and processes they used versus those that others' used. Students will begin to explore similarities and differences between the strategies and processes used.
Fifth Grade	Students will solidify their thinking on strategies and processes by making decisions on the most efficient way to solve problems. Stretching their thinking to realize that efficiency can be influenced by the perspective of the author/creator.

Standard 5

CCSS.Math.Practice.MP5: Use appropriate tools strategically.

2016 ISTE Student Standard: Computational Thinker 5b

Understanding the word around us is essential for adult success. Young children are continually taking input from their surroundings and trying to "make sense of it." Learning what tools help in solving mathematical problems correctly and efficiently will help our student to better understand and find success in our world.

*Mathematically proficient students **consider the available tools when solving a mathematical problem**. These **tools might include pencil and paper, concrete models, a ruler, a protractor, a calculator, a spreadsheet**, a computer algebra system, a statistical package, or dynamic geometry software. Proficient students are sufficiently familiar with tools appropriate for their grade or course to make sound decisions about when each of these tools might be helpful, recognizing both the insight to be gained and their limitations. For example, mathematically proficient high school students analyze graphs of functions and solutions generated using a graphing calculator.*

They detect possible errors by strategically using estimation and other mathematical knowledge. When making mathematical models, they know that technology can enable them to visualize the results of varying assumptions, explore consequences, and compare predictions with data.

Mathematically proficient students at various grade levels are able to identify relevant external mathematical resources, such as digital content located on a website, and use them to pose or solve problems. They are able to use technology tools to explore and deepen their understanding of concepts.

ISTE/CSTA COMPUTATIONAL THINKING VOCABULARY

Automation: Consider the available tools when solving a mathematical problem; tools might include pencil and paper, concrete models, a ruler, a protractor, a calculator, a spreadsheet

How to Teach It

Don't tell students what tool to use. Leaving the decision-making process in the hands of the student will possibly cause frustration, which is what teachers should want. This will lead to discussions about what tool worked best and why. Teachers should provide a variety of tools so that students can make choices and discover what works best for them.

K–5 Student Progression for Standard 5

Kindergarten	Students begin to consider available tools (including estimation). For example, students may use linking cubes to represent two quantities to compare them side-by-side.
First Grade	Students expand their knowledge of available tools. For example, they may first estimate and then use linking cubes, colored chips or a ten-frame to model an addition problem.
Second Grade	Students move into the representational stage by adding the use of graphic organizers. For example students may use a drawing of a ten-frame or tally marks, as well as concrete items.
Grades 3–5	Students will expand upon their tools with graph paper, rulers, calculators, protractors, compass, t-charts, Venn diagrams, fraction tiles, self-created graphic organizers, and so on.

Standard 6

CCSS.Math.Practice.MP6: Attend to precision.

2016 ISTE Student Standard: Computational Thinker 5b

How many teachers have opened an item to be assembled, only to discover that the directions in the box could not be easily followed? Being able to help our students explain themselves so that they can be understood is an essential component for helping them to be Career and/or College Ready.

Our current system has a fundamental flaw (Reinhart 2000) when teachers stand in front of the class demonstrating and explaining. It would behoove teachers to change their thinking of good teaching from, "one who explains things so well that students understand" to "one who gets students to explain things so well that they can be understood." This again suggests that teacher must create a learning environment that values risk-taking and making mistakes (Boaler & Dweck (2016).

Mathematically proficient students try to **communicate precisely** *to others. They try to* **use clear definitions** *in discussion with others and in their own reasoning. They* **state the meaning** *of symbols they choose, including the equal sign consistently and appropriately. They are careful about specifying units of measure, and labeling axes to clarify the correspondence with quantities in a problem. They calculate accurately and efficiently, express numerical answers with a degree of precision appropriate for the problem context. In the elementary grades, students give carefully formulated explanations to each other. By the time they reach high school they have learned to examine claims and make explicit use of definitions.*

ISTE/CSTA COMPUTATIONAL THINKING VOCABULARY

Data Collection: Use clear definitions

Data Analysis: State the meaning

Data Representation: Communicate precisely

How to Teach It

Ask good questions by focusing on process questions, rather than product questions. With pressures in the amount of content that teachers need to over, they often result to asking things like, "When you add 3 + 5, that will equal...?" and they wait for the students to respond back "8." These questions are much faster than asking students a process questions such as, "If you have 3 object and 5 objects, how many are there all together?"

K–5 Student Progression for Standard 6

Kindergarten	When students say, "I don't get it," they will begin to understand that they need to be clear and precise in the language they use in explaining what they "don't get."
Grades 1–2	Students will eliminate the use of "I don't get it," by replacing with clear and precise language. Teachers will continue to strengthen clear and precise mathematical language by having student explain their thinking in front of their peers. Teachers will ask clarifying questions that students can explain.
Grades 3–5	Students will expand upon their use of clear and precise language by specifying units of measure, meaning of symbols and appropriate labels for diagrams and graphs they create.

Standard 7

CCSS.Math.Practice.MP7: Look for and make use of structure.

2016 ISTE Student Standard: Computational Thinker 5d

Seeing things from multiple perspectives is a common theme throughout the Common Core State Standards in a variety of subject areas. Finding patterns and repeated reasoning helps students to create connections to help solve more complex problems. For example, when students learn about fact families, they come to understand that addition and subtraction is really about parts that make up a whole. In 8 - 3 = 5, 8 - 5 = 3, 3 + 5 = 8, and 5 + 3 = 8, eight represents the whole and three and five make up the parts.

*Mathematically proficient students look closely to **discern a pattern or structure**. Young students, for example, might notice that three and seven more is the same amount as seven and three more, or they may sort a collection of shapes according to how many sides the shapes have. Later, students will see 7 x 8 equals the well remembered 7 x 5 + 7 x 3, in preparation for learning the distributive property. In the expression $x^2 + 9x + 14$, older students can see the 14 as 2 x 7 and the 9 as 2 + 7. They recognize the significance of an existing line in a geometric figure and can use the strategy of drawing an auxiliary* *line for solving problems. They also can step back for an overview and shift perspective. They can **see complicated things**, such as some algebraic expressions, **as single objects or as being composed of several objects.***

ISTE/CSTA COMPUTATIONAL THINKING VOCABULARY

Data Analysis: Discern a pattern or structure

Parallelization: See complicated things as single objects or as being composed of several objects

How to Teach It

Help students find patterns and repeated reasoning that can be built upon and lead to solving more complex problems. As students get older and gain more experiences, they will learn more strategies and get better at breaking apart complex problems into pieces so that they can apply strategies they know to solve each piece.

K–5 Student Progression for Standard 7

Kindergarten	Students begin to discern number patterns and/or structure. For example students might recognize that all teen numbers start with a 1 and ends with numbers 0-9. They also begin to recognize that 2 + 3 = 5 and 3 + 2 = 5.
First Grade	Students recognize the communitive property of addition (9 + 5 = 14 and 5 + 9 = 14). They also work with recognizing groups of 5 and 10 within a group of numbers being added or subtracted. For example (4 + 6 + 4) = (10 + 4) = 14 or (9 − 11) = (29 − 10) - 1 = (19 − 1) = 18.
Second Grade	Students begin using the patterns and structure to develop fluency (mental math strategies). Using patterns and strategies such as making ten, fact families, and doubles helps students to develop this fluency with numbers.
Third Grade	Students look closely to discover patterns and structures that involve strategies to multiply and divide. They begin with repeated addition and repeated subtraction, but move on to begin using the commutative and distributive properties to develop efficiency and fluency.

Fourth Grade	Students look closely to discover patterns and structures that explain calculations, such as the partial products model. They relate representations of counting problems such as tree diagrams and arrays to the multiplication principal of counting. They will begin generating number and shape patterns that follow a given rule.
Fifth Grade	Students look closely to discover patterns and structures that use previously mastered properties of operations as strategies to add, subject, multiply and divide with whole numbers and begin applying the strategies to fractions and decimals.

Standard 8

CCSS.Math.Practice.MP8: Look for and express regularity in repeated reasoning.

2016 ISTE Student Standard: Computational Thinker 5a, 5d

Help students see the "big picture" of mathematics! Being able to generalize strategies, procedures and processes will help students in being able to solve real-world problems of any type in any context. For example, if students need to determine the surface area of a cylinder, they should not have to memorize the formula. Students should first understand that a cylinder is made up of a rectangle and two circles. In breaking down the object into their pieces and using prior knowledge of the area of rectangles and circles, students should be allowed to explore how their previous knowledge applies to finding the surface area of this new shape.

*Mathematically proficient students notice if **calculations are repeated**, and **look both for general methods and for shortcuts**. Upper elementary students might notice when dividing 25 by 11 that they are repeating the same calculations over and over again, and conclude they have a repeating decimal. By paying attention to the calculation of slope as they repeatedly check whether points are on the line through (1,2) with slope 3, middle school students might abstract the equation $(y-2) / (x-1) = 3$.*

*As they work to **solve a problem**, mathematically proficient students maintain oversight of the process, while attending to the details. They continually evaluate the reasonableness of their immediate results.*

Algorithm & Procedures: calculations are repeated, solve a problem

Automation: look both for general methods and for shortcuts

How to Teach It

Help students see the "big picture" of mathematics. Students should understand that the surface area of a cylinder is made up of a rectangle (with an area of $l \times w$) and 2 circles (with an area of). Going further they will need to understand that the rectangle width is the same as the height measurement in the original formula. More importantly the student will need to understand that the length of the rectangle is the distance around the circle (circumference). To find the circumference of the circle one must take the radius x 2 (diameter) multiplied by 3.14. Hopefully students also understand that represents the number of times the length of the radius will wrap around the entire circle. For example, if the diameter (the radius multiplied by 2) can be represented by a string 4 inches long, then the 4-inch string will wrap about the circle 3.14 times. That is a lot of understanding to be done! Khan Academy has a great video explanation of cylinder volume and surface area.

K–5 Student Progression for Standard 8

Kindergarten	Students notice repetitive actions in counting and computation. For example, students notice that the next number in a counting sequence is one more and when counting by tens that the next number in the sequence is ten more.
First Grade	Students begin to understand place value as they add and subtract numbers. They look for the use of tens and multiples of ten when adding and subtracting larger numbers. Students continually ask themselves, "Does this make sense?"

Second Grade	Students will use rounding strategies to round up or round down. Adjustments to compensate for the rounding will then occur. Teacher should intently look for this strategy and allow for mistakes as they work through the process.
Third Grade	Students begin to look for shortcut methods to build upon what they already know. For example, if a student is asked to find a product of 7 x 9, they might decompose the seven into a 5 and a 2. They can then work with 7 x 2 and 7 x 5 to arrive at 14 + 35 = 49.
Fourth Grade	Students will notice repetitive actions in computation to make generalizations. Students will use models to explain calculations and understand how algorithms work, as well as create their own algorithms. For example, the use of visual fraction models to create equivalent fractions.
Fifth Grade	Students will apply all these concepts to new domains when working with fractions and decimals. Exploration and understanding of area models for multiplication and division will help students verbally explain why basic algorithms work. Formulas will be understood through the decomposition of its parts.